The MILITARY HISTORY of
CIVIL WAR LAND BATTLES

The MILITARY HISTORY of

Civil War

Maps by Pictograph Corporation Graphic Syndicate, Inc.,
after sketches by the author

Decorations by Leonard Everett Fisher

Land Battles

by TREVOR NEVITT DUPUY
COLONEL, U.S. ARMY, RET.

Franklin Watts, Inc.

575 Lexington Avenue   New York 22, N.Y.

THE author and publisher wish to thank R. Ernest Dupuy, Colonel, U.S. Army, Ret., for his helpful suggestions regarding this book.

.

To Laura
—to help her know "all about the Civil War."

SBN 531-01253-0

Library of Congress Catalog Card Number: 60–5577

© COPYRIGHT 1960 BY FRANKLIN WATTS, INC.

Printed in the United States of America

12 13 14 15 16 17

CONTENTS

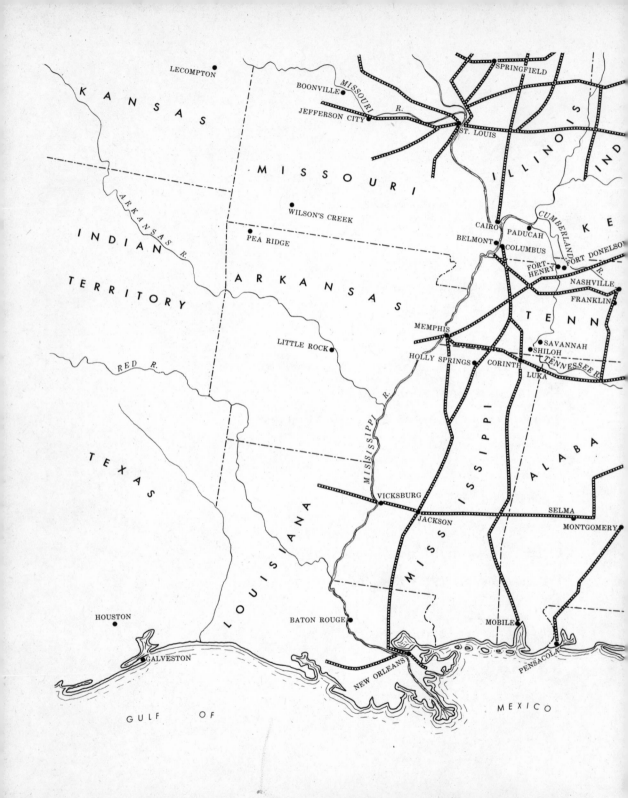

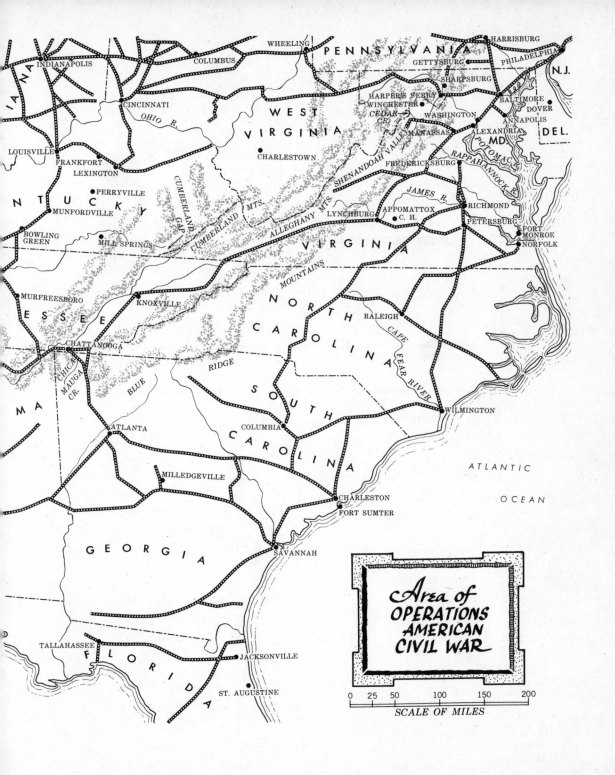

WHEELING
PENNSYLVANIA
HARRISBURG
GETTYSBURG
PHILADELPHIA
SHARPSBURG
N.J.
INDIANA
INDIANAPOLIS
COLUMBUS
WEST
VIRGINIA
HARPER'S FERRY
WINCHESTER
CEDAR CR.
WASHINGTON
BALTIMORE
DOVER
ANNAPOLIS
DEL.
CINCINNATI
OHIO R.
ALEXANDRIA
MD.
MANASSAS
POTOMAC R.
LOUISVILLE
CHARLESTOWN
SHENANDOAH VALLEY
FREDERICKSBURG
RAPPAHANNOCK R.
FRANKFORT
LEXINGTON
CUMBERLAND MTS.
ALLEGHANY MTS.
JAMES R.
RICHMOND
PERRYVILLE
LYNCHBURG
APPOMATTOX C. H.
PETERSBURG
KENTUCKY
MUNFORDVILLE
CUMBERLAND GAP
VIRGINIA
FORT MONROE
BOWLING GREEN
MILL SPRINGS
NORFOLK
MURFREESBORO
MOUNTAINS
KNOXVILLE
NORTH
TENNESSEE
RALEIGH
CHATTANOOGA
CAROLINA
CHICKAMAUGA CR.
RIDGE
CAPE FEAR RIVER
BLUE
SOUTH
ATLANTA
COLUMBIA
WILMINGTON
ALABAMA
CAROLINA
MILLEDGEVILLE
ATLANTIC
OCEAN
CHARLESTON
FORT SUMTER
GEORGIA
SAVANNAH
Area of
OPERATIONS
AMERICAN
CIVIL WAR
TALLAHASSEE
FLORIDA
JACKSONVILLE
ST. AUGUSTINE

0   25   50   100   150   200
SCALE OF MILES

Diagrams of Basic Attacks

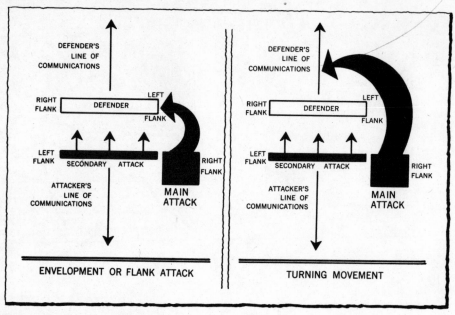

ENVELOPMENT OR FLANK ATTACK | TURNING MOVEMENT

Map Symbols Frequently Used

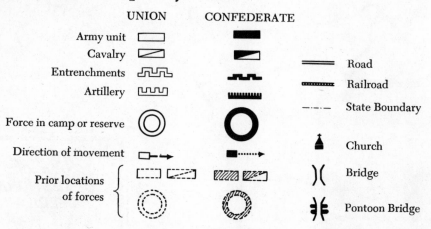

	UNION	CONFEDERATE
Army unit		
Cavalry		
Entrenchments		
Artillery		
Force in camp or reserve		
Direction of movement		
Prior locations of forces		

Road
Railroad
State Boundary
Church
Bridge
Pontoon Bridge

THE ARMIES AND THE BATTLES

To UNDERSTAND the land battles of the Civil War, we must know something about the armies that fought in that war, and the reason they were fighting each other.

In the years before 1860 there had been growing differences in the ways in which people lived, thought, and earned their livings in the Northern and Southern parts of the United States. One of the chief differences was in the people's feelings about slavery. Long before the Revolution, the planters in the South had discovered that in order to grow and harvest crops like tobacco and cotton, they would need many more people to work on the land. They got them by buying Negro slaves, brought by boat from Africa. For almost 250 years the economy of the South had been built around the use of these slaves on the big plantations. Most slave-owners treated their slaves kindly, but did not think it wrong to own, buy, and sell human beings like farm animals. This was the way they and their slaves had always lived, and their parents and grandparents before them. Even some of those Southerners who didn't like the idea of slavery felt that it could not be stopped without upsetting the Southern economy and way of life.

In the North, the farms were smaller and grew more varied crops. Slavery was not needed and had been outlawed in many Northern states. Most Northerners thought slavery was evil, and didn't consider the problems which would exist in the South if slavery were abolished. This made Southerners angry, because it was mostly Northern merchants who had grown rich by bringing slaves from Africa in years gone by. There was constant friction over slavery.

There were other frictions, too. Life in the agricultural South was different from life in the industrial North. People even thought differently. As factories brought more people and greater wealth to the Northern states, Southerners began to fear Northern domination. Many decided that they should leave the Union and establish their own country.

In 1860 these Southerners decided that the time had come to leave the United States. Abraham Lincoln, a Northern Republican opposed to slavery, had been elected President. In December, a little more than a month after the election, South Carolina declared it was seceding—or withdrawing—from the Union. Then in April 1861, South Carolina decided to seize Fort Sumter, held by Union troops, on an island in Charleston harbor. Fort Sumter surrendered on April 13, after a two-day bombardment. President Lincoln called upon the other states to help put down this rebellion. The Northern states responded, but nearly all of the Southern states decided to join South Carolina.

By June, 1861, eleven Southern states had seceded from the Union and established the Confederate States of America, with its capital at Richmond, Virginia. Confederate President Jefferson Davis expected the Union government would try to force the South to return to the Union, and had built up an army to keep this from happening.

Lincoln was just as determined to preserve the Union. The Confederate attack on Fort Sumter showed him that the South would fight for its new independence. So he called for volunteers to increase the tiny Regular Army of 16,000 men.

The first armies that met in battle that year were composed almost entirely of cheerful young men who had no idea of what war was like. They knew nothing of the discipline and training needed for effective fighting. Only a few of the officers knew more than their men.

At the beginning of 1861, there had been about 1,000 officers in the regular army. Most of them had gone to school at West Point. Many had fought in the Mexican War, and against the Indians. About a third of these leaders were Southerners who resigned from the Regular Army to join the Confederacy.

So the first battles of the war were fought between armies composed mostly of untrained recruits, led on both sides by a handful of experienced officers. With such leadership the recruits sometimes fought well, but they lacked discipline. Sometimes they ran away in the middle of a battle despite all the efforts of their officers to rally them.

By midsummer of 1862, after much marching, drilling, and fighting, the inexperienced officers and men had become veterans. The great armies which fought the remaining three years of the war were as fine as any the world had ever seen.

The Union armies were more numerous than those of the Confederacy. For every two young men of fighting age in the South, there were five such men in the North. But this was not as serious a disadvantage for the Confederacy as it might seem. In order to win the war, Southerners merely had to stay on the defensive and repel Northern attacks. The North, however, could win the war only by invading the South, defeating the Confederate armies, and establishing absolute military control over every bit of rebellious territory.

Experienced military men on both sides knew that when the forces of each are about equal in experience and ability, it takes many more men to attack successfully than to hold a defensive position. Considering the different tasks of the two sides, military men estimated that they were almost perfectly matched regarding the number of men each needed.

In the end the North won the war mainly because of its economic strength and its successful blockade of the Southern coast. But almost to the very end of the war there seemed to be a chance the Confederates would win if they could discourage the North from continuing the fight.

MILITARY TERMS USED IN THIS BOOK

DEPLOY: To spread out to make a battle line.

DIVERSION (*also* DEMONSTRATION): Act of drawing the attention and force of an enemy from the point of the chief military operation.

ENVELOPMENT: An attack against the flank of the enemy army.

FLANKS: The sides of the army's line as it goes into battle.

HOLDING (*also* SECONDARY) ATTACK: A small attack to divert the enemy from the point of the chief military operation.

LINE OF COMMUNICATIONS: The route by which supplies and reinforcements reach a fighting army. It can be a road, a railroad, or often both.

MAIN ATTACK (*also* EFFORT): A big, concentrated attack against a weak or critical point.

TURNING MOVEMENT: A movement around the enemy's flank to attack his line of communications in the rear of his battle line.

BULL RUN, OR MANASSAS

July 21, 1861

ON A BRIGHT Sunday morning in July, 1861, crowds of picnickers rode in carriages and on horseback along the dusty road from Washington, D.C., toward Centerville, Virginia. They had heard that General Irvin McDowell's Union army would march from Centerville that day to sweep aside the rebels near Manassas Junction, a few miles further south. The picnickers intended to see the fun.

As they neared Centerville, they saw occasional groups of soldiers marching back toward Washington. These were some of the men who had volunteered for three months service on April 15, 1861 shortly after the fall of Fort Sumter. Their time was up, and they were going home.

13

In the next few days, the term of service would expire for most of McDowell's remaining 30,000 men. Although he knew they were not yet ready for battle, McDowell had to fight while he still had an army. He ordered an attack early on that morning of July 21.

There were about 20,000 Confederates near Manassas, protecting the main railroad lines leading to the important regions of Virginia. These men, commanded by General Pierre Beauregard, held a line along Bull Run, a small stream between Manassas Junction and Centerville. Like McDowell's troops, they were almost all inexperienced recruits.

Beauregard had been in command of the Southern troops which had captured Fort Sumter three months earlier. He was a former Regular Army officer, from Louisiana, who had resigned to join the Confederacy. He and McDowell had graduated from West Point together in 1838. Now they were enemies, commanding armies about to fight a great battle.

Another small Southern army, about 12,000 strong, was located in the Shenandoah Valley, near Winchester. This was commanded by General Joseph Johnston, another former Regular Army officer. Union General Robert Patterson, with 18,000 men, was supposed to keep Johnston busy in the Valley while McDowell attacked Beauregard.

Johnston learned of McDowell's plan to attack, and knew that Beauregard's troops would be greatly outnumbered. Daringly, he moved his entire army from the Shenandoah Valley to Manassas, completely fooling Patterson, who didn't learn about the move until later. Johnston's men went by train—the first time an army had ever moved to battle by railroad. By morning of July 21, the

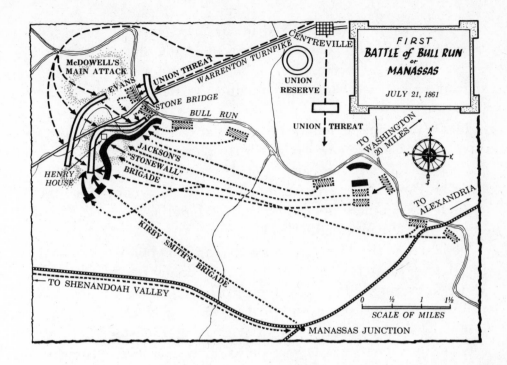

FIRST
BATTLE of BULL RUN
or
MANASSAS

JULY 21, 1861

better part of Johnston's army had reached Manassas. One brigade was still on the railroad and would arrive about noon.

General Johnston ranked higher than Beauregard, so he took command of the combined Southern armies. But since Beauregard had made most of the plans for battle, Johnston left the younger general in direct control of the fighting.

The fighting began soon after dawn with a Union attack on the Confederate left flank, where the Warrenton Turnpike crossed Bull Run over a stone bridge. General Nathan Evans, who commanded Southern troops near the Stone Bridge, drove back the attack without much trouble. Then Evans looked behind him to see great clouds of dust, kicked up by marching feet. It looked as if a great body of Union troops was making a surprise envelopment. Evans sent a message to Johnston and Beauregard and quickly took most of his men to stop the Unionists north of the Turnpike.

McDowell himself led this main attack of most of his army against the Confederate left flank. He pushed back Evans's brigade easily. Evans was soon joined by neighboring units, and then by General Beauregard and some of the troops from the right of the Southern line. But even so the outnumbered Confederates were driven steadily back.

Just south of the Turnpike was a large, rolling hill. It was called the Henry House Hill because the Henry family lived in a farmhouse in the broad field at the crest. Here Beauregard set up a new line to stop McDowell. In the center of it was a brigade commanded by another Southern West Pointer, General Thomas Jackson. Jackson's brigade was known as the best drilled unit in the Confederate Army.

Meanwhile Evans's men and their neighbors were beginning to run away. Evans and the commander of a South Carolina brigade, General Barnard Bee, tried in vain to rally them. Then Bee, looking back, saw Jackson's men drawn up in soldierly array along the top of the Henry House Hill. At this impressive sight he turned to his men and shouted, "There stands Jackson like a stone wall! Rally behind the Virginians!"

The Union troops pressed on, but Jackson's brigade stayed as firm as the stone wall to which Bee had compared it. From then on it was always known as the "Stonewall Brigade," and its commander has gone down in history as "Stonewall" Jackson.

For more than three hours the fight raged for the Henry House Hill. The inexperienced soldiers on both sides fought bravely, but by mid-afternoon it looked as though the Northerners would win. Jackson's brigade held its line, but the Union troops began to push back the Confederate left flank.

Then the train carrying Johnston's last brigade arrived at Manassas Junction. These men, Texans commanded by General Edwin Kirby-Smith, unloaded immediately and hurried to join the fight. They struck the right flank of the advancing Northerners.

This was too much for McDowell's tired men. His whole line panicked. In a few minutes all the Union troops were in flight back across Bull Run.

The untrained Confederates were in no condition to follow. They had barely escaped disaster themselves. A few Confederates did try to harass the retreating troops, and increased Union panic with accurate fire from one cannon. To add to the confusion, the picnickers were now trying desperately to get back to Washington.

Marching calmly behind the terrified mob was a single battalion of Union soldiers commanded by Major George Sykes. These were Regular Army soldiers—experienced, disciplined, and obedient to orders. Stray musket and cannon balls did not bother them. These few men discouraged the Southern attempts at pursuit.

The defeat at Bull Run showed the North that the Union could be preserved only by a long and costly war, and then only if its soldiers could fight like Sykes's Regulars. Confederate leaders realized that they, too, needed better-trained men. But above all, the Battle of Bull Run, or Manassas, had given the South reason to hope for an early victory.

FORT DONELSON AND SHILOH

February 12–16 and April 6–7, 1862

WEST OF THE Appalachian Mountains, both North and South wanted to gain control of Missouri and Kentucky, border states. These were slave states, but the people who lived in them were almost equally divided in their feelings between loyalty to the Union and sympathy for the Confederacy.

Young General Nathaniel Lyon had established Union authority over most of Missouri before he met a hero's death at the Battle of Wilson's Creek in southwest Missouri, August 10, 1861. But things had gone more slowly in Kentucky, which tried to be neutral in the war. By the end of August neither Northern nor Southern soldiers had entered Kentucky, although troops of both sides were massed along its borders.

Early in September, General Albert Sidney Johnston, in command of Confederate troops west of the Appalachians, advanced from Tennessee into Kentucky. Johnston was a former Regular Army officer who had had a brilliant military career. Seizing Columbus and Bowling Green, he moved his troops rapidly in an effort to capture Paducah and Smithland, where the Tennessee and Cumberland rivers joined the Ohio. But General Ulysses S. Grant, who commanded Union troops in southern Illinois, had already seized the two towns. Both sides watched each other warily for several months.

Grant tried to get the approval of cautious General Henry Halleck, over-all Union commander in the West, for an advance into Kentucky to break General Johnston's line. He was supported by crusty old Commodore Andrew Foote, who commanded the Union navy's gunboats on the Ohio and Mississippi rivers. Halleck finally agreed to their proposed army-navy expedition up the rivers of western Kentucky, and early in February, 1862, Grant and Foote started.

Johnston had expected this, and had built two forts to block the Tennessee and Cumberland rivers. The one on the Tennessee was called Fort Henry. Fort Donelson, larger and stronger, was twelve miles away on the Cumberland.

But the Confederates were not prepared for the speed and energy of the Union commanders. Grant and Foote moved against Fort Henry on February 6. As soon as Grant's soldiers unloaded on the river bank, Commodore Foote attacked the fort with his gunboats. After a terrible pounding from the Union navy guns, the fort surrendered before the soldiers got into the fight.

Grant immediately moved against Fort Donelson, where General John B. Floyd was in command, assisted by Generals Gideon Pillow and Simon Buckner. Under them were 15,000 men. Johnston had been sure they could hold the fort almost indefinitely.

Neither Floyd nor Pillow were experienced soldiers, and they became panicky after a noisy but unsuccessful bombardment by Foote's gunboats on February 14. Next day, instead of holding the fort, the Southerners tried to fight their way out. They shattered the Union right flank in a surprise attack, but the three Southern generals got into an argument and failed to take advantage of their chance to escape. Grant launched a counterattack which swept through the outlying entrenchments, and Northern soldiers pushed right to the walls of the fort.

Floyd and Pillow made a cowardly escape up the river, leaving their men and General Buckner to face defeat. During the night Buckner sent a message to Grant suggesting an armistice to discuss terms for surrender. Grant promptly replied in words that would make him famous: "No terms except an unconditional and immediate surrender can be accepted. I propose to move immediately upon your works."

Buckner had been at West Point with Grant, and they had served together as Regular Army officers before the war. Knowing that Grant meant what he said, Buckner surrendered unconditionally on February 16.

Johnston now had to withdraw from Kentucky. He tried to form a new line in Tennessee, but Grant and General Don Carlos Buell, in command of Union forces in eastern Tennessee, pushed quickly behind the retreating Southerners to seize Nashville on February 25. With his army hopelessly split by this advance, Johnston was now forced to move further back, and he concentrated his forces

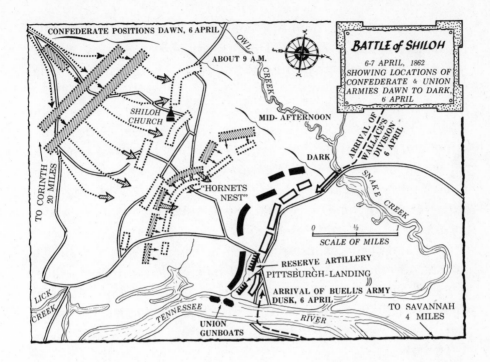

CONFEDERATE POSITIONS DAWN, 6 APRIL

OWL CREEK

ABOUT 9 A.M.

SHILOH CHURCH

MID-AFTERNOON

TO CORINTH 20 MILES

DARK

"HORNETS NEST"

BATTLE of SHILOH

6-7 APRIL, 1862
SHOWING LOCATIONS OF
CONFEDERATE & UNION
ARMIES DAWN TO DARK,
6 APRIL

ARRIVAL OF WALLACE'S DIVISION 6 APRIL

SNAKE CREEK

0   ½   1
SCALE OF MILES

RESERVE ARTILLERY
PITTSBURGH-LANDING
ARRIVAL OF BUELL'S ARMY
DUSK, 6 APRIL

TO SAVANNAH 4 MILES

LICK CREEK

TENNESSEE   RIVER

UNION GUNBOATS

in southwestern Tennessee and northeastern Mississippi. By late
March he had assembled about 40,000 men in the neighborhood
of Corinth, Mississippi, an important railway junction.

Meanwhile, Grant had pushed rapidly up the Tennessee River
to the vicinity of Savannah, Tennessee. He had planned to move
on to Corinth, in northern Mississippi, and could have reached it
before Johnston if Halleck had not ordered him to wait near
Savannah until Buell arrived from Nashville. From March 11 until
early April, Grant and his 40,000 men were camped along the
banks of the Tennessee between Savannah, Pittsburg Landing,
and nearby Shiloh Church.

21

Johnston, with the help of General Beauregard, used this time to reorganize his discouraged troops. By the evening of April 5, he had secretly assembled his army near the Union camp at Shiloh Church.

Surprisingly, the Union army did not realize that General Johnston had moved 40,000 men into the woods in front of their lines. Grant and his generals were a bit too sure of themselves. Johnston's repeated retreats through Kentucky and Tennessee made them think that he would never attack. When the Confederate army struck at dawn, Sunday, April 6, the Northerners were completely surprised.

Grant, fearlessly exposing himself to a hail of Southern bullets, managed to reorganize his men, but they could not halt the determined Confederate advance. Grant had ordered one of his six divisions, only five miles away, to march at once to the battlefield. But this division got lost in the woods and did not arrive until after dark.

By mid-afternoon, Grant knew that his line was cracking in the face of the Confederate attack. Ordering his men to stand fast as long as they could, he established a new line about a mile and a half to the rear, behind a stream which flowed into the river at Pittsburg Landing. While his soldiers held the "Hornets' Nest" against repeated attacks, Grant scraped together odds and ends of units, and a great number of stragglers who had wandered away during the fight. Most important, he collected all of his available artillery, and massed these guns on a hill overlooking the stream. Then he ordered his troops to fall back to this line.

Now it was the Confederates' turn to be surprised. Blasted from the front by Grant's powerful new artillery line, they found themselves hit from the flank by the big guns of two Union gunboats on the river. They were thrown back with great loss from Grant's last-ditch position.

This was the end of that Sunday's fighting. The Southern troops now learned that General Johnston had been killed leading a charge against the "Hornets' Nest." Perhaps worst of all, those on the right flank could see boats ferrying Northern soldiers from the eastern bank of the river. General Buell's army had arrived at last, and 20,000 fresh men were ready to fight for the Union next day.

Beauregard, who had taken command after Johnston's death, tried hard to reorganize his troops. But he had only a few hours of darkness, in a terrible rainstorm, to get ready for the Union attack he expected early Monday morning.

Grant, assisted by Buell, was also busy during that dismal night, preparing for the next day's battle. Shortly after dawn his troops attacked, and this time they pushed the Confederates back. Although the Southerns fought as bravely as the Northerners had fought the day before, they had no reinforcements to call on. There was no way Beauregard could establish a new reserve line, as Grant had done, to save the battle. By noon of April 7, the Confederates had been driven back beyond Shiloh Church. Hopelessly defeated, they began to retreat down the road to Corinth. The Battle of Shiloh was over.

"THE VALLEY"

May–June, 1862

IN THE EAST, much had happened since July, 1861. Thirty-five-year-old General George B. McClellan had been brought to Washington to take command of the army that had been defeated at Bull Run. McClellan was a West Pointer who had distinguished himself in the Mexican War. Soon thereafter he resigned from the army, but when the Civil War broke out, he immediately volunteered, and became a Major General in the Union army. He had been chosen for his important new job because he had won several small victories in West Virginia at the start of the war.

McClellan reorganized the Union army, now called the Army of the Potomac. As new recruits arrived at Washington, he quickly made them into proud soldiers, physically fit, fully equipped, and ready to fight. In a short time he proved himself one of the great military organizers of history.

But as the summer months turned into fall, and winter came, McClellan's army stayed in its camps and on its drill fields near Washington. The Northern people began to wonder why McClellan did not move against General "Joe" Johnston, whose army still held the Bull Run battlefield. McClellan insisted that his army was not ready, and that the Southern army was much larger than his own. The fact was, Johnston had less than half as many troops as McClellan.

Finally, in March, 1862, President Lincoln insisted that McClellan make some move, and make it immediately. McClellan suggested that he take his army down the Potomac River by steamboat and land it in eastern Virginia. In this way he would by-pass the Confederate army and actually be closer to Richmond than Johnston was at Manassas. McClellan believed that if he could capture the Southern capital, the Confederacy would collapse and the war would soon be over.

President Lincoln, with some misgivings, approved McClellan's plan, but insisted that McDowell's corps should be left behind to protect the Union capital. Otherwise, he pointed out, while McClellan's army was heading toward Richmond, Johnston might march thirty miles to capture Washington. He agreed that McDowell and his 40,000 men would march overland to join McClellan after the Army of the Potomac had arrived near Richmond.

Late in March, McClellan began to transport his army to Fort Monroe, at the tip of Virginia's "Peninsula." Even though he had 100,000 men, and opposition was weak, his progress up the Peninsula was very slow. Finally, by mid-May, his soldiers could see the church steeples of Richmond. But Johnston's army was already securely entrenched to defend the Confederate capital. McClellan, still exaggerating Confederate strength, refused to attack before McDowell arrived.

Meanwhile, President Davis's military adviser, General Robert E. Lee, suggested that if a few Confederate troops were to make a big stir in northern Virginia, McDowell might never arrive to reinforce McClellan. The Union government would keep him there to protect Washington. Lee suggested that General "Stonewall" Jackson should carry out this diversion in the Shenandoah Valley.

For several months Jackson, with less than 5,000 men, had been making things uncomfortable for the Union army in the northern part of the Valley. He had so worried the Northern government that they had sent an army of 20,000 men, under General Nathaniel P. Banks, to drive him south. Late in April, in order to carry out Lee's plan, Jackson was given reinforcements that brought his strength up to 17,000 men.

Before carrying out Lee's orders, however, Jackson wanted to make sure the Northern army in western Virginia would not interfere with him. Union General John C. Frémont had about 10,000 men in the mountains just west of the Shenandoah Valley. Jackson felt that a good scare would take care of Frémont.

On May 8, 1862, Jackson appeared at the mountain village of McDowell where the right flank of General Frémont's army overlooked the approaches to the Shenandoah Valley. Jackson smashed the Northerners, and sent them scurrying back into western Virginia.

Jackson now marched rapidly northward to the region where

26

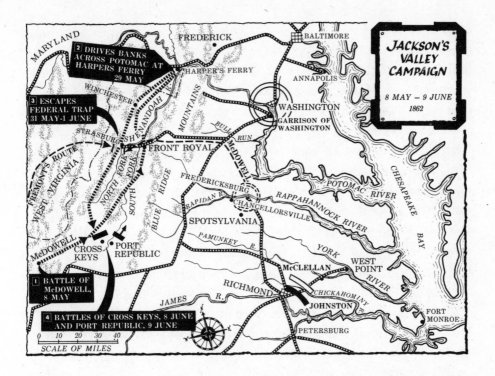

the Valley is split by the Massanutten Mountains. General Banks retreated in front of him to Strasburg and Front Royal, just north of these mountains. "Stonewall" now pretended to move down the western passage of the Valley, along the North Fork of the Shenandoah River, to threaten Strasburg. But on May 23, marching with the speed that earned his soldiers the nickname of "foot cavalry," Jackson crossed over the Massanutten Mountains and attacked the Unionists at Front Royal.

It was a short fight. General Banks and his army streamed northward in confusion, back to their base at Winchester. Jackson followed at once. On May 25, there was another short, decisive fight at Winchester. Jackson chased Banks out of Winchester and right across the Potomac River into Maryland. By May 29, Jackson had reached the outskirts of Harper's Ferry, having captured quantities of equipment and weapons abandoned by the Northerners. These were collected in a tremendous wagon train.

Jackson's amazing move down the Valley had come just as McDowell was about to march south from Fredericksburg to join McClellan. Immediately McDowell was ordered to change his plans and hurry to the Shenandoah Valley to try to block Jackson's line of withdrawal from Harper's Ferry. At the same time, General Frémont was ordered to march eastward from the other side of the Valley, to join McDowell in the vicinity of Strasburg and Front Royal. General Banks was given reinforcements, and told to try to drive Jackson southward into this trap.

Calmly, but rapidly, Jackson began marching south again. With him, and protected by his entire army, went his wagon train of captured Northern equipment.

By evening of May 29, Frémont's advanced guard was less than 20 miles from Strasburg, while McDowell's leading division, commanded by General James Shields, was a scant ten miles east of Front Royal. Jackson's army was more than thirty miles north of these towns! It seemed certain that in a few hours his line of retreat would be blocked by overwhelming numbers.

But Jackson's "foot cavalry" sped southward. On May 31, the head of his column pushed between Frémont and Shields at Strasburg. He sent blocking forces in both directions to hold off the Northerners. Before the two Union commanders could assemble enough men to push back these flank guards, Jackson's long column had slipped through the trap, right under the eyes of North-

28

erners on both sides of the road. He didn't lose a single wagon from his train of booty.

Jackson continued to march up the Valley. Frémont followed up the North Fork of the Shenandoah, while Shields marched up the South Fork, between the Massanutten and Blue Ridge mountains. By the night of June 7, the two Northern generals again seemed to be closing in on Jackson. He was camped near the towns of Cross Keys and Port Republic, just south of the Massanutten Mountains, apparently making no effort to escape.

Early on June 8, Frémont, who had succeeded in bringing up 12,000 men, attacked Jackson's left flank at Cross Keys. Jackson had only 6,500 men at Cross Keys, but he had a low opinion of Frémont, and a high opinion of his own men and of his left flank commander, General Richard Ewell. As Jackson sat on his horse, quietly watching the battle, he knew that he had not been mistaken. His veterans threw back the Northern attack easily.

Sure that Frémont would do nothing more for several days, Jackson turned against Shields's division of 10,000 men. Early on June 9 he attacked with 15,000 men and, although the Northerners resisted strongly, he drove Shields back down the South Fork of the Shenandoah. Jackson had brought the Valley Campaign to a glorious conclusion just one month and a day after it had begun at the Battle of McDowell.

Lee's plan had been carried out perfectly. With only 17,000 men Jackson had thrown the North into panic, and tied up 70,000 Union troops. McDowell's corps never reached the important region of operations near Richmond. McClellan's army sat waiting for reinforcements that never came.

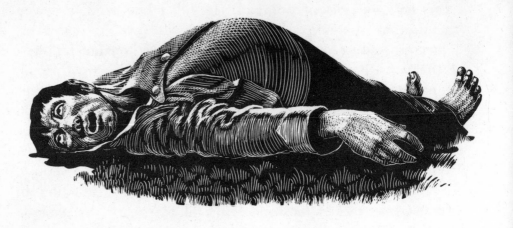

SEVEN DAYS' BATTLE

June 26–July 2, 1862

BY MAY 25, 1862, McClellan, with his Army of the Potomac, had reached the vicinity of Richmond. Still believing that "Joe" Johnston's entrenched army was larger than his own, McClellan made no effort to attack. He deployed his army on either side of the Chickahominy River about five miles east of Richmond, and waited for reinforcements.

McClellan did not like to have his army split by a river. He knew that an enemy could attack one part and possibly defeat it before the rest of the army could get into the fight. Yet he needed a strong position south of the river as a base for attack when McDowell's corps arrived, and he needed a force on the north bank to prevent interference with the arrival of these reinforcements, and to help protect his line of communications along the railroad east of Richmond. (Food, ammunition, and other equipment were being landed from ships at West Point, Virginia, on the York River, and collected in a great supply depot at nearby White House, on the railroad line from West Point to Richmond.) So, to make the best possible connection between the two parts of his army, McClellan had several bridges built across the Chickahominy.

Johnston decided to try to take advantage of this division of the Union army. He knew that there were about 60,000 Union troops north of the river near Mechanicsville and Cold Harbor, about 20,000 to the south near Fair Oaks and Seven Pines, and 20,000 in reserve. His own army numbered a little more than 60,-000 men. General John B. Magruder, with less than 20,000 men, would make a noisy demonstration against the Northern army's right wing, pretending to attack across the Chickahominy. At the same time, Johnston with about 45,000, would attack the 20,000 Union soldiers near Fair Oaks.

Johnston struck on May 31. Magruder's demonstration kept the Union right wing pinned down, but Johnston's main attack did not go well. Inexperienced officers had trouble coordinating the battlefield movements of great numbers of untrained men. Though the fighting was fierce, and lasted a day and a half, there was never enough Confederate strength at one point to push through the Union defenses, and McClellan was able to send reinforcements to the threatened spot.

Johnston was seriously wounded late on May 31. The loss of this capable general might have been disastrous for the South, but for one thing: President Davis decided to have his own mili-

31

tary adviser, General Lee, take Johnston's place. When Lee took command on June 1, he gave the army a new name: the Army of Northern Virginia. And he immediately began to work out a new plan to defeat the Army of the Potomac.

Early in June, McClellan shifted his troops so that he had about 60,000 men south of the Chickahominy, leaving 30,000 north of the stream. Lee, like Johnston, decided to try to take advantage of this division of the Union army. He sent for "Stonewall" Jackson, who had just finished his Valley Campaign, and for other reinforcements. Lee's army grew to 90,000 men, almost equalling McClellan's.

Union General Fitz-John Porter's corps, 30,000 strong, was north of the Chickahominy. Lee planned to strike Porter with about 65,000 men, leaving only 25,000 under General John B. Magruder to demonstrate against the 60,000 Unionists south of the stream.

Magruder's demonstration on June 26 was successful, but things didn't go well north of the Chickahominy. Partly it was the same old trouble—the officers hadn't yet learned how to coordinate the movements of thousands of troops in a big attack. But it was also due to the exhaustion of Jackson and his men, who had not had time to rest from the Valley Campaign before making the long trip to Richmond.

Jackson was supposed to get behind Porter's right flank and attack from the rear, while Lee's men attacked from the front at Mechanicsville. But Jackson didn't reach the battlefield, and Lee's men couldn't break Porter's line.

That night Porter learned that Jackson was in a position to move behind him, so before dawn he moved back to a new position

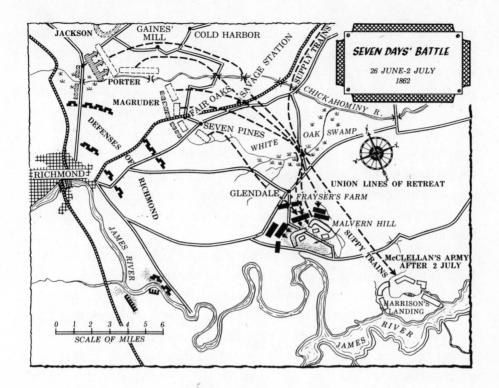

near Gaines's Mill. Lee attacked again on June 27, with the same plan as the day before. Again Jackson was slow, but once he arrived, the Confederates were able to drive Porter from his positions, and nearly pushed the Union troops into the Chickahominy. Then, at dusk, Northern reinforcements arrived over the bridges, and Porter's line held.

Less than half of the Union army had been engaged, and they had fought well. But McClellan decided the battle was lost. He ordered a retreat, and started to move his supply base to the south side of the Peninsula on the James River where he could be sup-

33

ported by Union navy guns. Had he been half as bold as Lee, he might still have won a great victory, for Magruder had only a thin line of troops in front of Richmond, south of the Chickahominy. If McClellan had pushed hard, as some of his generals urged him, he could have captured Richmond on June 27 or 28. But though his army wasn't defeated, McClellan was a beaten man.

When Lee found part of the Northern army retreating on June 28, he suspected a trick. He followed slowly and got ready to attack again next day. When he discovered that the entire Army of the Potomac was retreating to the James River, he ordered an immediate pursuit.

But McClellan had left General Edwin V. Sumner's corps in a delaying position at Savage Station, on the railroad south of the Chickahominy. Sumner repulsed several fierce attacks by Magruder. Having to rebuild the bridges across the Chickahominy, destroyed earlier by Union troops, Jackson was delayed and so didn't arrive till dark. By this time Sumner had done his job of delaying the Southern troops. He moved south after the rest of the Union army.

Meanwhile, Confederate Generals James Longstreet and A. P. Hill had rushed south from Gaines's Mill to try to cut off the Union retreat. They were stopped by a line of Northerners in defensive positions running from White Oak Swamp through Glendale to Malvern Hill. On June 30, the rest of McClellan's army, with its long train of supplies, streamed south behind this line, while the Union rear guard delayed Jackson's pursuit across White Oak Swamp. That night the Union army withdrew to new defensive positions on Malvern Hill.

Next day, July 1, the Union army stayed on Malvern Hill while the Union supply trains reached Harrison's Landing on the James River. Here in an area almost impossible to attack, surrounded by swamps and water, and protected by the guns of the Union navy, they established a new base.

That afternoon the Southerners struck again, but they couldn't make any progress up the open slopes of Malvern Hill in the face of overwhelming Northern artillery fire. Lee suffered more than 5,000 casualties, while the Union army lost less than 2,000. But instead of counterattacking the tired Southerners, McClellan retreated again next day, back to the safety of the new base at Harrison's Landing.

The Seven Days' Battle, lasting from June 26 to July 2, had been an amazing conflict. The Northerners had repelled every Confederate attack, though they had been close to defeat at Gaines's Mill on June 27. Union killed and wounded totaled less than 10,000 men, while the Southerners had lost more than 16,000. Yet when the battle was over the Confederacy was jubilant, the North glum. The threat to Richmond was ended. The invading army was huddled in its entrenchments twenty miles away.

The battle had proved that there wasn't much, if any, difference between the fighting qualities of the two armies. But one of the generals, Lee, had confidence in his men and in himself; the other, McClellan, did not. And that is why the Seven Days' Battle is remembered as a Southern victory.

SECOND BULL RUN, OR SECOND MANASSAS

August 29–30, 1862

WHILE MCCLELLAN'S ARMY of the Potomac was retreating across the Virginia Peninsula in the Seven Days' Battle, a new Northern army took to the field further north. This was the Army of Virginia, 55,000 strong, commanded by General John Pope. Pope established a large supply base at Manassas, scene of the war's first battle, and deployed his army along the line of the Rappahannock River. By mid-July he was ready to push southward toward Richmond.

Lee was now between two Union armies which, combined, had double his strength of about 75,000 men. Afraid that McClellan would advance against Richmond from his new base at Harrison's Landing, Lee held most of his army near the city, but sent Jackson with about 24,000 men to hold Pope north of the Rapidan River.

. In early August, Lee could see that McClellan's army was about to be sent back north from Harrison's Landing by boat. He suspected that it would reinforce Pope for an overland drive to Richmond. Once these two Union armies were united, Lee was afraid that he would be overwhelmed.

Lee decided to try to defeat Pope's army before it could be reinforced. Though McClellan was still at Harrison's Landing, Lee left only about 20,000 men to defend Richmond, and moved to join Jackson. By August 24, Lee, with 55,000 men had reached Brandy Station, just south of the Rappahannock. There he learned that Union transports were moving McClellan's army from Har-

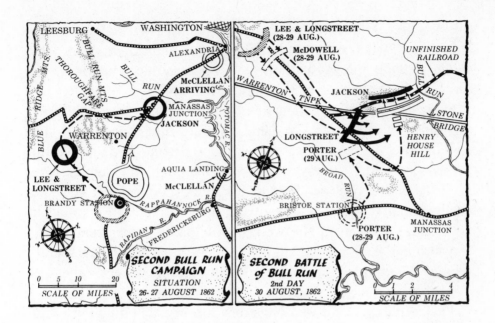

LEESBURG · WASHINGTON
ALEXANDRIA
BULL RUN MTS.
THOROUGHFARE GAP
BLUE RIDGE MTS.
BULL RUN
McCLELLAN ARRIVING
MANASSAS JUNCTION
JACKSON
WARRENTON
POTOMAC R.
LEE & LONGSTREET
POPE
AQUIA LANDING
McCLELLAN
BRANDY STATION
RAPPAHANNOCK R.
RAPIDAN R.
FREDERICKSBURG

SECOND BULL RUN CAMPAIGN
SITUATION
26-27 AUGUST 1862
0 5 10 20
SCALE OF MILES

LEE & LONGSTREET (28-29 AUG.)
McDOWELL (28-29 AUG.)
UNFINISHED RAILROAD
WARRENTON TNPK
JACKSON
BULL RUN
STONE BRIDGE
LONGSTREET
PORTER (29 AUG.)
HENRY HOUSE HILL
BROAD RUN
BRISTOE STATION
PORTER (28-29 AUG.)
MANASSAS JUNCTION

SECOND BATTLE of BULL RUN
2nd DAY
30 AUGUST, 1862
0 1 2 4
SCALE OF MILES

rison's Landing to Acquia Landing and Alexandria, on the Potomac. In another week he would be faced by nearly 150,000 men. He must defeat Pope before McClellan's troops arrived.

Lee now ordered one of the boldest military movements in history. On August 25 he sent Jackson's corps northwest, between the Blue Ridge and Bull Run mountains, to cross the Bull Run Mountains through Thoroughfare Gap and seize Manassas Junction. Lee followed next day with Longstreet's corps.

Jackson and his men were now well rested. In two days they marched fifty-four miles, and by evening of August 26 they had reached the Union supply depot at Manassas. The Union Army of Virginia was completely cut off from Washington.

Pope, as Lee had expected, rushed his forces north to deal with this new development. The Union general knew that Jackson had only about 20,000 men and he felt sure he could overwhelm Jackson, or drive him away without too much trouble. Then he would turn and beat the rest of the Southern army.

Meanwhile Jackson's men spent all of August 27 re-equipping themselves from the great Union stores, then burned all they couldn't use. Jackson had no intention of letting Pope attack him before Lee and Longstreet arrived. That night he put his corps in a defensive position behind an unfinished railroad cut just northwest of the Henry House Hill and the old Bull Run battlefield. Here, hidden in the woods, in a ready-made trench, they stayed quietly all day on August 28. Pope's troops went marching around the countryside, looking for the vanished Southerners.

That evening Lee and Longstreet reached Thoroughfare Gap, where some Union troops under General McDowell were posted. A few miles to the southeast, near Bristoe's Station, was Porter's corps—the first part of McClellan's army to arrive from the Peninsula. Porter and McDowell teamed up to block any further advances by Longstreet, and sent a message to tell General Pope what they had done.

To distract attention from Longstreet's approach, Jackson now revealed his hiding place by firing on a Northern unit that was marching past. This worked even better than he had hoped. Pope became so excited that he refused to believe Longstreet was approaching, and ordered Porter and McDowell to attack Jackson's right flank at once.

McDowell obeyed Pope's order, but Porter realized that such a move would permit Longstreet to attack the rear of Union troops facing Jackson. He continued to face west, delaying the advance of

38

Longstreet and Lee until late on August 29, when Longstreet succeeded in moving up beside Jackson. Lee now had 48,000 men on the battlefield, while Pope had about 60,000. But McClellan's men were on the way. Lee ordered Longstreet to attack next day to push Porter aside.

Pope had been attacking Jackson all day with most of his army, but had been repulsed each time. That evening he learned that Porter had not obeyed his order. He was furious, since he still did not believe that Longstreet was near. He ordered Porter to move at once to join the next morning's attack on Jackson. Porter obeyed the order. He knew he had done his best to protect the Union flank, and that if disaster resulted, it would be Pope's fault.

When Longstreet moved forward on August 30, he found Porter gone. The Southerners swept ahead without opposition until they struck the rear of the left wing of Pope's army. At the same time, Jackson counterattacked from the front. Most of the Union army was thrown into confusion.

Some of the Union troops were able to reorganize and slow down the Southern attack, but they couldn't stop it. They were driven back across Henry House Hill to the Stone Bridge and Bull Run. Sykes's division of Porter's corps acted as a rear guard to cover the stream crossings as the Union army retreated northeastward to Washington. This was the same Sykes who had commanded the Union rear guard at the First Battle of Bull Run.

Once more the South had won a great victory on the Manassas battlefield. They had lost 9,000 men in the battle, but inflicted more than 15,000 Union casualties. This was partly because the Northern commander, Pope, had been foolishly stubborn. But the victory was mostly due to the generalship of Robert E. Lee, and the teamwork of his corps commanders.

39

ANTIETAM, OR SHARPSBURG

September 17, 1862

AFTER HIS VICTORY at Manassas, Lee decided to invade the North. He hoped this would so discourage the Northern people that they might make peace with the Confederacy. Also, Lee and President Davis hoped that a great Confederate victory would encourage England and France to help the South win the war. The English and French governments were sympathetic to the Southern cause, and the Union blockade of the South was causing great economic distress in England. Mills were idle and thousands of people out of work because of the lack of Southern cotton.

On September 4, 1862, Lee began to cross the Potomac into Maryland. By September 7, he had reached Frederick, where he rested briefly. He had slightly less than 50,000 men and he hoped to capture Harrisburg, capital of Pennsylvania. But first he wanted to move his line of communications west to a safer location, in the Shenandoah and Antietam valleys. To do this, he would have to capture Harper's Ferry, where the Shenandoah River flows into the Potomac. Harper's Ferry was held by 12,000 Union troops.

Lee planned a bold division of his small army. He ordered Jackson's corps to go back across the Potomac River to seize Harper's Ferry. Part of Longstreet's corps would help Jackson by holding the heights above the town on the Maryland side of the river. With the rest of Longstreet's corps, less than 20,000 men, Lee would go north to Hagerstown. They started on September 9.

Meanwhile, the panic-stricken North did not know where Lee would strike next. In the crisis, President Lincoln again turned to McClellan to lead the army. The soldiers trusted McClellan, and soon were ready to fight again. McClellan started northwest from Washington on September 10 with 90,000 men.

On September 13, McClellan had a tremendous stroke of luck. While marching through Frederick, his soldiers found a copy of Lee's order to Jackson and Longstreet. So McClellan learned that the Southern army would be scattered over thirty miles, with parts on both sides of the Potomac.

Midway between the widely separated portions of Lee's army was the town of Sharpsburg, Maryland. McClellan's advance troops had already reached the eastern slopes of South Mountain, only about eight miles from Sharpsburg, and the rest of the army was close behind. There were only weak Confederate outposts holding the mountain passes. Part of McClellan's army could have reached Sharpsburg on September 13.

Had McClellan been bolder and quicker, the war might have

41

ended in September, 1862. But he waited until September 14 to drive the Southerners from the South Mountain passes, and didn't cross with his main army until the next day. Even so, he still could have overwhelmed Lee, who had now moved to Sharpsburg with 25,000 men. McClellan could have brought at least 50,000 men into battle on September 15, and 70,000 or more on September 16. But instead of attacking, he slowly assembled his army on the east bank of Antietam Creek.

Meanwhile, Jackson captured Harper's Ferry on September 15. Leaving A. P. Hill's division to take charge of prisoners and the large store of captured supplies, Jackson made a rapid night march to join Lee at Sharpsburg, early on September 16. Hill was to follow as soon as possible.

McClellan finally decided to attack the next day. He planned to strike early in the morning against the Confederate left flank, following soon afterward with a crushing blow against the right flank, south of Sharpsburg.

But McClellan's orders were not clear. There was no coordination between his units. One corps, under the command of "Fighting Joe" Hooker, attacked at dawn, and pushed Jackson's left flank back for about half a mile. But Lee sent reinforcements from other parts of the line, and Jackson stopped Hooker after both sides had suffered severe losses. Then, about mid-morning, Sumner's corps attacked the Confederates a little further south. Again Lee and Jackson rushed reinforcements from other parts of the line. A dreadful struggle took place, centered on a road afterwards known as the "Bloody Lane." Finally the Northerners were stopped, after they had gained some ground.

General Ambrose Burnside, on the Union left, did not try to

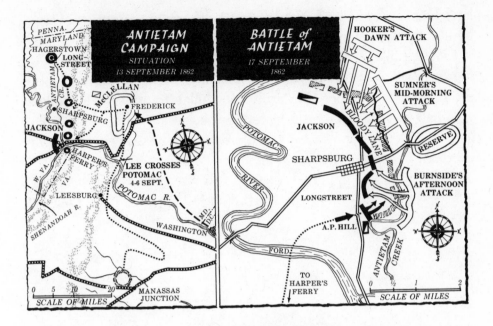

attack the Confederate line until afternoon. Once started, however, he advanced rapidly because Longstreet had been weakened by sending help to Jackson in the morning. Then, just as the Northerners were driving the Confederates back into Sharpsburg, Southern General A. P. Hill's division arrived from Harper's Ferry, and struck Burnside's left flank. The Northerners were forced back to the creek. The Battle of Antietam, the bloodiest day of the Civil War, was over.

But it shouldn't have been. The Southerners were exhausted and couldn't have resisted another big attack. McClellan had 20,-000 fresh troops in reserve, and the troops that had fought that morning could have tried again. Lee's army had its back to the river, and could have been destroyed. Victory had lain in McClellan's hands ever since he had found Lee's orders. Time after time he had thrown away his chance.

Lee had lost 13,500 in killed and wounded in that awful day of fighting, yet with about 32,000 exhausted men, he stayed in his position on September 18, daring McClellan to attack. McClellan, who had lost 12,500 men, reacted as Lee was sure he would. He had 70,000 men, 20,000 of them fresh, but he stayed where he was, not accepting Lee's challenge.

That night Lee quietly slipped away and recrossed the Potomac. His first invasion of the North had failed. But so had General McClellan.

PERRYVILLE AND STONES RIVER, OR MURFREESBORO

October 8, 1862, and December 31–January 3, 1862–63

IN MARCH, 1862, General Halleck was given command of the Union armies in the West. In April he came to Shiloh, shortly after the battle, to take personal command of the combined armies of Grant and Buell, nearly 100,000 men. Confederate General Beauregard, with 35,000 men, held the important railroad junction of Corinth, Mississippi, only twenty-one miles to the southwest of Shiloh. But Halleck moved so cautiously that it took his army a month to cover that short distance, giving Beauregard plenty of time to move all of his supplies south to a new position before he abandoned Corinth to the Northerners. At this time Beauregard became ill, and General Braxton Bragg, who had fought bravely as a corps commander at Shiloh, took his place.

After taking Corinth, Halleck sent General Buell with about 50,000 men to capture Chattanooga, the gateway to Georgia and Alabama, two hundred miles to the east. But Buell moved slowly, and the rest of Halleck's troops remained inactive near Memphis and Corinth. Bragg then rushed most of his army to Chattanooga. Though he had started later, and had further to go, he reached Chattanooga before Buell, who took positions twenty miles northwest of the city.

Since Bragg had about 50,000 men, counting General Kirby-Smith's 15,000 at Knoxville, he decided to make a daring move. He would march past Buell's army through Tennessee and into

Kentucky. He hoped he could get enough recruits in northern Tennessee and Kentucky to recapture both states for the Confederacy. He and Kirby-Smith started in mid-August, 1862. As the army marched north, Confederate cavalry commanders, General Nathan B. Forrest and Colonel John H. Morgan, cut telegraph lines and destroyed railroads behind the Union armies.

The Southern invasion of Kentucky dismayed the North. Buell followed Bragg—but at a safe distance. Finally, in late September, while the Confederates were living off the country and collecting recruits in northern Kentucky, Buell reached Louisville, where he received reinforcements.

Then Buell got word that he would be replaced as soon as the Union government found a better general. To save his job, he marched southeast with 60,000 men on October 3, looking for Bragg's army. Four days later his advanced guard ran into Confederate outposts just west of Perryville.

Only 16,000 Southerners, parts of two corps commanded by Generals Leonidas Polk and William J. Hardee, were at Perryville when the Union army arrived. But early on October 8, the Confederates attacked, and almost drove the Northerners off the field. More Union troops marched up to join the battle, however, and by the end of the day two-thirds of Buell's army had gotten into the fight. During the last hours of the fight, 1,200 Southern cavalrymen, under young General Joseph Wheeler, demonstrated so actively on the Confederate left flank that a Union division of more than 15,000 took up defensive positions, thinking they were going to be attacked by superior numbers.

So, though neither side won the Battle of Perryville, the glory was almost entirely with the Southerners, who came near to beat-

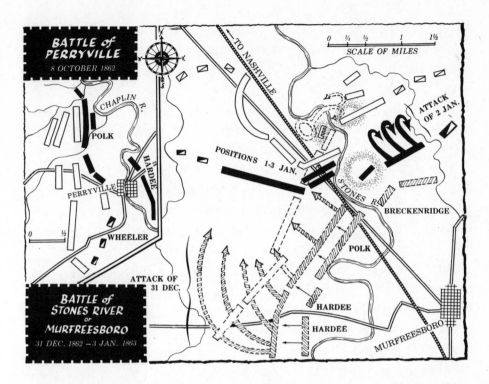

BATTLE of PERRYVILLE
8 OCTOBER 1862

CHAPLIN R.
POLK
PERRYVILLE
HARDEE
WHEELER

0   ½   1
ATTACK OF 31 DEC.

BATTLE of STONES RIVER or MURFREESBORO
31 DEC. 1862 – 3 JAN. 1863

0   ¼   ½   1   1½
SCALE OF MILES

TO NASHVILLE
POSITIONS 1-3 JAN.
STONES R.
ATTACK OF 2 JAN.
BRECKENRIDGE
POLK
HARDEE
HARDEE
MURFREESBORO

ing a force more than twice as large as their own. Wisely, they withdrew that night before Buell could attack with his whole army.

If Buell had followed quickly, he could have struck Bragg before the Southern army was concentrated for battle. But he didn't move, and by October 10 Bragg was ready for him.

Now Bragg should have attacked. Though both armies were nearly the same strength, Bragg's troops were almost all tough veterans, while Buell had many new men. But, to the disgust of his officers and men, Bragg retreated back to Tennessee.

Again Buell didn't follow. This time he really did lose his command. On October 30, General William S. Rosecrans took his place.

47

Rosecrans quickly moved the army to Nashville, then became as cautious as Buell. For almost two months he stayed at Nashville, saying that he needed the time to reorganize his army and collect supplies.

Meanwhile, Bragg had gotten back some of his old confidence and moved his army to Murfreesboro, thirty miles south of Nashville. He had about 38,000 veteran troops.

The day after Christmas, Rosecrans finally moved south from Nashville with 44,000 men, and reached the Confederate outposts northwest of Murfreesboro on December 29. By evening of December 30, his army was concentrated for battle just west of Stones River.

Bragg's army was entrenched on both sides of the stream, covering the roads and railroads leading into Murfreesboro. Three-fourths of the Southern army was west of the river. Bragg knew it was dangerous to split his army this way, but there were many fords and bridges over the stream, and he planned to keep the Northerners so busy that they would not have a chance to concentrate against either part of his army.

Strangely enough, each commander planned to envelop the other's right flank on December 31. Bragg ordered Hardee's corps to strike the Union right flank at dawn. Then, with Polk joining the attack, the Southern army would act like a great swinging door, sweeping the Northerners right back into Stones River.

Rosecrans planned to send part of General Thomas Crittenden's corps across the river early on December 31, to hit General John Breckinridge's division north of Murfreesboro. The remainder of the Union army would make a holding attack to keep the Confederates busy west of the river.

Crittenden's men had barely started across the river when they were called back. The Northern right flank had been shattered in a surprise dawn attack by Hardee's corps, and Crittenden's men were needed to try to stop the Confederate advance.

The Union line was pushed back five miles by Hardee's and Polk's men, practically into the river, as Bragg had planned. Rosecrans put every available man into the fight, and finally the attackers were stopped just short of the Nashville turnpike, the vital Northern supply route. Late in the day Bragg brought Breckinridge's division across the river to join the attack, but the Union lines now held firm.

On New Years Day, 1863, both sides were too exhausted to start fighting again. Rosecrans sent some troops to the east side of the river to protect his rear, and to assure a line of retreat if necessary. On January 2, he moved more troops to the east bank.

Afraid that the Northerners might try to move on Murfreesboro and hit the Southern right flank, Bragg sent Breckinridge back across the river to attack them, but the Northerners were ready. Assisted by a powerful collection of artillery on the west bank, the Union defenders east of the stream repulsed the Confederate attack with heavy losses.

This ended the battle of Stones River, or Murfreesboro. Both armies were quiet on January 3, but that evening Bragg withdrew to new positions further south. Union losses had been 12,900 men. Confederate casualties were 11,700.

By his withdrawal, Bragg granted the victory to Rosecrans. The battle had not decided anything, but in Northern minds it helped make up for a disaster that had just taken place in Virginia.

FREDERICKSBURG

December 13, 1862

PRESIDENT LINCOLN HAD been disappointed when McClellan failed to destroy Lee's army at Antietam, but he was grateful to the general for having stopped the Confederate invasion of the North. For six weeks he waited for McClellan to use his superior strength to carry the war to the South. When, by November 7, 1862, McClellan still had not advanced against Lee, even Lincoln's patience was exhausted. He relieved McClellan of his command, and appointed General Ambrose Burnside to command the Army of the Potomac.

Burnside had proven himself a sincere, loyal man, who would not shrink from a fight. Yet this, perhaps, was not a very good quality in a man of limited intelligence. Burnside did not seem to know when he had a chance of winning a battle and when he did not. Since McClellan had been dismissed for not fighting, Burnside was determined to fight as soon as possible. He planned to cross the Rappahannock River at Fredericksburg, Virginia, and then to march south directly toward Richmond. He rightly figured that such an advance would bring him into conflict with Lee. Burnside had about 125,000 men, but he left 20,000 of them guarding his lines of communication.

Lee's army had been greatly reinforced since Antietam. Jackson with about 40,000 men, was guarding the Shenandoah Valley, while Longstreet, with the same number, was watching over the crossings of the upper Rappahannock. Lee planned to unite the army at whatever point was threatened by a Union advance. When Burnside moved from Warrenton toward the lower Rappahannock, Lee ordered Longstreet to shift over near Fredericksburg, and alerted Jackson to be ready to march.

When Burnside reached the river opposite Fredericksburg on November 17, he could have crossed it and seized the town and the heights beyond almost without opposition. But he decided to wait for his engineers to bring up pontons—boats for building floating bridges. The pontons did not arrive until December 9.

Meanwhile Lee ordered Longstreet to the heights west of Fredericksburg to watch the Union movements. At first Lee did not think any general would be foolish enough to try to assault those heights for they were held by well-equipped, proven soldiers. But as Union troops and equipment were massed on the far bank of the river, Lee realized that Burnside really thought he could attack successfully. Lee immediately sent for Jackson, and made ready for battle.

Some 73,000 Confederate veterans were entrenched on the heights overlooking Fredericksburg and the plain just south of the town. Two hundred and fifty guns had been placed to cover the river crossings and the town, and to sweep the fields to the south. One Confederate officer said that "a chicken could not live" on the ground dominated by that artillery.

Burnside did not try to bypass this concentration of firepower. On December 12 his men began to cross the river, driving the Confederate outposts out of Fredericksburg. Under the cover of Union artillery lining the left bank of the river, Union engineers built five ponton bridges.

Early on December 13, the attack began. It was bad enough to order such an assault at all, but Burnside made it worse by making two widely separated attacks, instead of one concentrated, main effort. Then, because his orders were not clear, and the various divisions acted independently, those separate attacks became a series of uncoordinated jabs instead of the powerful hammer blows that might have been successful.

The troops advancing through Fredericksburg to attack Longstreet's position on Marye's Heights never had a chance. They made attack after attack, only to be swept back each time by overwhelming firepower.

On the Union left, protected somewhat by trees and underbrush, General George G. Meade's division did for a time penetrate Jackson's position. But "Stonewall" quickly counterattacked to drive the Northerners back. By nightfall the Union army, badly shattered, had drawn back to the river's edge.

Burnside did not realize that his army had lost nearly 13,000 men in eight hours. He was about to order a second attack on

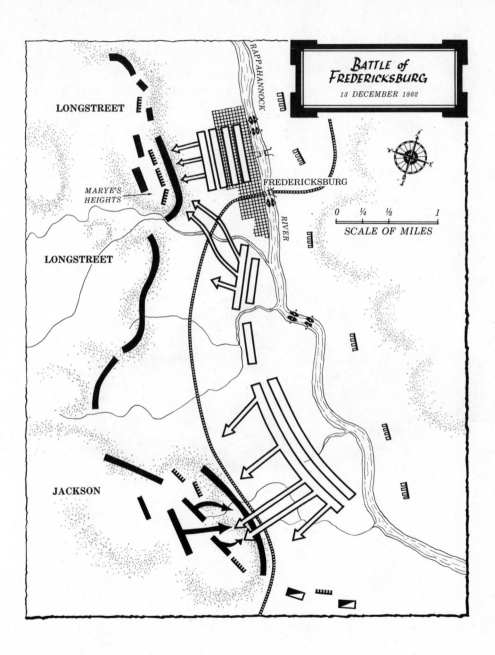

LONGSTREET

MARYE'S
HEIGHTS

LONGSTREET

JACKSON

RAPPAHANNOCK

FREDERICKSBURG

RIVER

BATTLE of
FREDERICKSBURG
13 DECEMBER 1862

0   ¼   ½   1
SCALE OF MILES

December 14, but his corps and division commanders persuaded him not to murder any more of his brave troops. The two armies held their positions the next day. Lee, who had lost about 5,300 men, did not counterattack because the Northern army still greatly outnumbered his own, and was protected by a powerful concentration of artillery lining the far bank of the river.

Burnside began to withdraw his army across the river on December 15, bringing to a close the brief, disastrous Fredericksburg campaign.

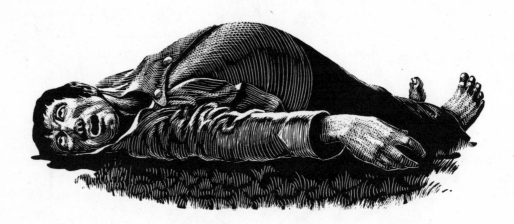

CHANCELLORSVILLE

May 1–6, 1863

BOTH THE GOVERNMENT and the Army of the Potomac lost confidence in General Burnside after his failure at Fredericksburg. In his place, President Lincoln appointed General Joseph Hooker.

"Fighting Joe" Hooker was known as a hard-fighting, skillful corps commander. Although he had a reputation as an ambitious trouble-maker, Lincoln was willing to risk his shortcomings if he could "go forward and give us victories."

Hooker reorganized the army, and soon restored to the troops some of the confidence they had lost at Fredericksburg. By the end of April, 1863, his 120,000 men were ready for combat. "My plans are perfect," he said. "May God have mercy on General Lee, for I will have none."

The Army of the Potomac had spent the winter in camps northeast of Fredericksburg, while the Confederate Army of Northern Virginia had remained near the positions it had successfully defended against Burnside. But in the spring Lee sent Longstreet, with two divisions, to gather supplies in southeastern Virginia. This left only about 60,000 Confederates near Fredericksburg.

Hooker's plan was to take about 75,000 of his men in a turning movement around Lee's left flank. Meanwhile, 45,000 men under General John Sedgwick would make a holding attack to keep Lee's army pinned down at Fredericksburg. If done with enough speed and skill, this nutcracker movement would force Lee to withdraw from Fredericksburg, or be surrounded.

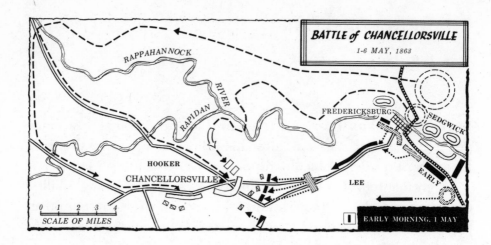

BATTLE of CHANCELLORSVILLE
1-6 MAY, 1863

RAPPAHANNOCK

RAPIDAN RIVER

FREDERICKSBURG

SEDGWICK

HOOKER

CHANCELLORSVILLE

EARLY

LEE

0 1 2 3 4
SCALE OF MILES

EARLY MORNING, 1 MAY

Hooker's plan started well. On April 30 his main army began to cross the Rappahannock and Rapidan rivers in three columns, and the advanced troops reached Chancellorsville. Meanwhile, Sedgwick crossed the river near Fredericksburg and began his holding attack.

Lee was too good a general not to realize that he was about to be caught in a trap. Even so, he wasn't going to let Hooker have Fredericksburg without a fight. He left General Jubal Early with less than 15,000 men, to hold the Fredericksburg heights against Sedgwick. Then he took Jackson and the remainder of his army, about 45,000 men, to stop Hooker to the west.

On May 1, pushing east from Chancellorsville, Hooker ran into Lee's advance guard. Though the Northerners were much more numerous than the Southerners, Hooker halted the advance and ordered his men to dig defensive entrenchments. Hooker's plan had been excellent, but now he had stage fright.

As soon as Lee saw that the Northerners had stopped their ad-

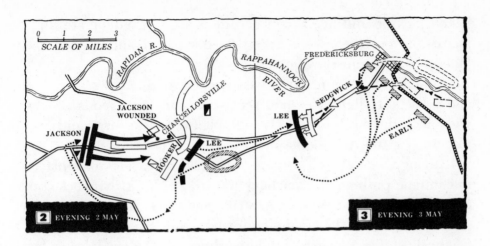

SCALE OF MILES

0 1 2 3

RAPIDAN R.

RAPPAHANNOCK RIVER

FREDERICKSBURG

JACKSON WOUNDED

CHANCELLORSVILLE

SEDGWICK

JACKSON

LEE

LEE

HOOKER

EARLY

2 EVENING 2 MAY

3 EVENING 3 MAY

vance, he decided to attack! That evening he outlined to Jackson one of the most brilliant war plans in all the history of warfare. While Lee held the line east of Chancellorsville with less than 20,000 men, Jackson's corps, 26,000 strong, would make a long march westward early on May 2, then turn east to strike behind the Union right flank. A battle that had started as a Union turning movement around Lee's left flank was to become a Southern envelopment of Hooker's right flank. Lee was actually planning an encirclement of an army twice the size of his own!

Lee's plan worked perfectly, with Jackson's assistance. While Jackson marched more than twelve miles westward, Lee kept Hooker's 73,000 men pinned to their trenches. When Jackson attacked at 6:00 P.M., Hooker's right flank collapsed completely. By dark, Jackson's men had advanced three miles, almost to Hooker's headquarters at Chancellorsville.

Jackson now halted, preparing to continue the attack at dawn. With some of his staff he rode ahead to locate the Union positions.

When Jackson and his officers returned to the Confederate lines, guards mistook them for a Union cavalry patrol, and opened fire. Jackson was seriously wounded.

The entire Southern army was shocked at this news, but they had a battle to fight. Lee had received word that General Sedgwick had driven Jubal Early out of Fredericksburg, and was threatening the rear of the main Confederate army.

Leaving General "Jeb" Stuart (who had taken Jackson's place) to continue pushing Hooker back toward the Rappahannock, Lee and 20,000 men turned east to strike Sedgwick. The Northerners still outnumbered the Confederates by about two-to-one, both at Chancellorsville and near Fredericksburg. But when Hooker lost his nerve, his army lost its spirit. On the other hand, the Southerners fought with a gallantry that matched the great heart and will of their commander. By May 6, both parts of the Union army had been driven completely over the Rappahannock and Lee had won his greatest victory.

But at what a cost! Though they had inflicted losses of 16,800 on the Northerners, Lee's own men had suffered 12,800 casualties in the desperate fighting. Lee had also lost his "right hand." "Stonewall" Jackson died on May 10, of the wounds inflicted by his own troops. He was a brave, pious soldier to the end as he said quietly: "Let us cross over the river, and rest under the shade of the trees."

GETTYSBURG

July 1–3, 1863

A MONTH AFTER Chancellorsville, Lee was again ready to take the offensive. He and the Confederate government felt that now was the time to invade the North. They hoped that a successful invasion would make the discouraged Northerners agree to Confederate independence. And even if the Union continued fighting, more Southern victories might still encourage England and France to help the Confederacy.

Early in June, 1863, Lee began to move his army of 76,000 men quietly westward from Fredericksburg toward the Shenandoah Valley. From here he marched northward, crossing the Potomac near Sharpsburg, and on into Pennsylvania. The alarmed Union government ordered Hooker to move north, keeping east of the

Blue Ridge Mountains to protect Washington and other vital centers on the East coast which Lee might attack.

By June 28, the government in Washington was close to panic. The Southern army held Chambersburg, York, and Carlisle, with advanced troops threatening Harrisburg and Lancaster. "Jeb" Stuart's cavalry division had crossed the Potomac in sight of Washington, and was raiding northward between Hooker's army and Baltimore.

But it was no longer Hooker's army. He, too, had failed against Lee and had been replaced. Now General George Meade was in command of the Army of the Potomac, now near Frederick, Maryland.

Meade continued northeast, toward Hanover and York, to keep between Lee and Washington. With Stuart's cavalry off on its raid, Lee's army had lost its "eyes." Not knowing where Meade was, or when he might push in between the scattered Southern units, Lee now called back his leading divisions from Carlisle and York, and concentrated his army near Cashtown. He had decided to wait for Stuart, and then to beat the Northern army, before continuing with his invasion.

Meanwhile Meade moved cautiously northward toward Hanover and Emmitsburg. His cavalry was out front, making a screen between the Union troops and Southern scouts while it tried to find out where the Southerners were and what they planned to do.

Late on June 30, a Confederate brigade looking for supplies marched southeast down the Gettysburg-Cashtown road. Just northwest of Gettysburg they ran into Union cavalry outposts. So it happened that the site of the greatest battle ever fought on American soil was chosen by chance.

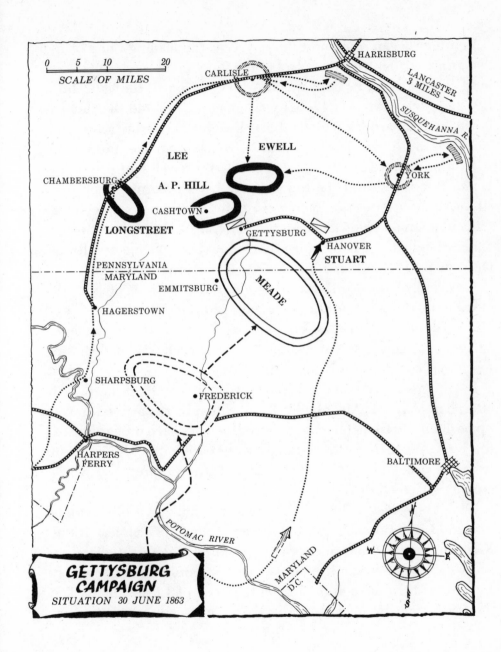

SCALE OF MILES
0 5 10 20

HARRISBURG

LANCASTER
3 MILES

CARLISLE

SUSQUEHANNA R.

LEE

EWELL

A. P. HILL

CHAMBERSBURG

YORK

CASHTOWN

LONGSTREET

GETTYSBURG

HANOVER

STUART

PENNSYLVANIA

MARYLAND

EMMITSBURG

MEADE

HAGERSTOWN

SHARPSBURG

FREDERICK

HARPERS
FERRY

BALTIMORE

POTOMAC RIVER

MARYLAND
D.C.

N

S

GETTYSBURG CAMPAIGN
SITUATION 30 JUNE 1863

Fighting began in earnest on July 1, as the leading units of the two armies struggled for control of the junction of roads at Gettysburg. The battle grew fiercer as nearby units joined the fight. Both Lee and Meade, realizing what was going on, ordered the concentration of their armies at Gettysburg, the Northern army advancing from the south, the Southern army arriving from the north.

By afternoon, the corps of A. P. Hill and Ewell had driven the Union troops south of the town. Here the Northerners took up a strong defensive position facing north and northwest on Cemetery Hill. The Union right flank units held Culp's Hill, while the left flank stretched out southward along low-lying Cemetery Ridge. On a map, the Northern line looked like a great fishhook.

Lee, finding the Northern army gathering in front of him, decided to mount a major attack the next morning. While Ewell and Hill made secondary attacks from the locations they then held, Longstreet's corps, still marching to the battlefield, would swing south and envelop the Union left flank.

But Longstreet's units were not ready for an attack until early afternoon of July 2. Meanwhile, more Union troops arrived to take up positions on Cemetery Ridge, and also in a peach orchard just to the west. When Longstreet attacked, he swept the Union troops from the peach orchard, but was halted by well-prepared Northerners on Cemetery Ridge.

Now Longstreet's right flank began to climb two hills, Round Top and Little Round Top, at the southern end of Cemetery Ridge. From these hills the Confederates would have dominated the entire Union position, and the envelopment would have been easy. But just as they were approaching the crest of Little Round Top, they were met by unexpected artillery and small arms fire.

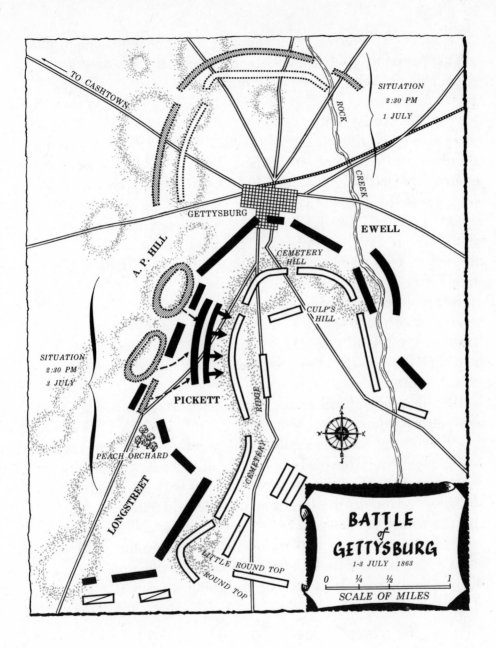

TO CASHTOWN

SITUATION
2:30 PM
1 JULY

ROCK

CREEK

GETTYSBURG

EWELL

A. P. HILL

CEMETERY
HILL

CULP'S
HILL

SITUATION
2:30 PM
3 JULY

PICKETT

CEMETERY RIDGE

PEACH ORCHARD

LONGSTREET

N

LITTLE ROUND TOP

ROUND TOP

BATTLE
of
GETTYSBURG
1-3 JULY 1863

0   ¼   ½   1

SCALE OF MILES

General G. K. Warren, chief engineer officer of the Union army, had happened to climb Little Round Top just as Longstreet's men began their attack on the peach orchard. He saw the danger if the Confederates reached the tops of these two hills. He dashed down to Cemetery Ridge and, in General Meade's name, led the two nearest brigades to the crest of Little Round Top. Arriving just ahead of Longstreet's men, these brigades held their positions against repeated Southern assaults. Thanks to Warren the North did not lose the battle of Gettysburg on July 2. And Meade could also have thanked Ewell, who failed to keep pressure on the Union right flank as Lee had ordered. This permitted the Union commander to send the reinforcements which finally halted Longstreet's attack on the Round Tops at dusk.

Next day Lee decided to use some 15,000 fresh troops to assault the center of the Union line on Cemetery Ridge, where the defenders were spread thin. He assembled 160 cannon opposite this point, and early in the afternoon the Confederate artillery began a violent bombardment of the Union center.

After an hour of bombardment, the Southern guns had used up most of their ammunition. Now came the infantry's turn. In a long line, they swept into the shallow valley between the two armies. Battle flags flying, bayonets twinkling in the sun, the advancing Southern troops filled the silent Northerners with awe, admiration, and some terror. In the forefront was General Pickett's division, and this attack is known to history as Pickett's Charge.

Suddenly, the Union artillery opened fire. More than 200 guns, firing as fast as they could, tore great holes in the attacking lines. But the Southerners kept coming, marching steadily into the face of the murderous fire.

Then Northern musketry began to add to the slaughter. Some of the Confederates faltered, but most of the survivors, heads down as though walking into a high wind, continued up the Ridge. Right to the top they climbed, to engage the defenders in hand-to-hand combat. But Meade was ready for them. The Northerners counterattacked, and this was too much. The Confederates staggered back down the hill, to suffer more losses from the Union artillery.

Lee had watched the attack first with admiration, then with horror. Lee the General had made the worst mistake of his military career. But Lee the man had never been greater than when he rode up to the returning soldiers and said: "All this has been *my* fault—it is I that have lost this fight. You must help me out of it the best way you can."

Now, though his heart was heavy with grief, Lee skillfully withdrew his troops from the battle, and retreated back to the Potomac and into Virginia. Meade should have pursued, but the Union general and his men, thankful for their first clear victory over the Army of Northern Virginia, were content to let the Southerners withdraw without interference.

Meade, who had suffered 23,000 casualties, had shown that at last the Army of the Potomac had a capable, if not brilliant, commander. Lee had lost 28,000 men out of 75,000—one-quarter of these in less than an hour during Pickett's Charge. The tide of Southern victory was receding as Lee's army returned to Virginia.

VICKSBURG

April 30–July 4, 1863

IN JULY, 1862, General Halleck, commanding the Union armies in the west, had been called to Washington to become the General-in-Chief, President Lincoln's principal military adviser. He turned over command of the army near Corinth and Memphis to General Grant.

With only 42,000 men, Grant was expected to hold Memphis and Corinth, and to keep open long lines of communication through Tennessee and Kentucky to Illinois. The Confederates tried to take advantage of his weakness, but he defeated General Sterling Price at Iuka, Mississippi, in September, and then repulsed Price and General Earl Van Dorn at Corinth early in October.

When Grant received reinforcements later in the fall, he decided to advance to capture Vicksburg, Mississippi, the last important Confederate position on the Mississippi River. But as he moved further south, he found it harder and harder to protect his lengthening lines of communication against Confederate raiders. On December 20, General Van Dorn captured Grant's main supply base at Holly Springs, Mississippi. At the same time, General Forrest was attacking Grant's supply lines in northern Tennessee.

This was enough to convince Grant that he should try something different. Since the Union Navy controlled the Mississippi River north of Vicksburg, he could use the river as a line of communications that couldn't be cut by Southern raiders. Already a part of his army was at Milliken's Bend, Louisiana, on the river near Vicksburg. Early in January, 1863, Grant moved down to join them with the rest of his available field forces, keeping Memphis as his base.

Vicksburg was a powerful fortress whose guns dominated the river from a cliff 250 feet high. It could not be attacked from the front, and Grant knew that he could not try any other approach until winter and spring flood waters subsided. For three months he waited, keeping some of his men busy digging a canal to bypass the fortress, and sending others to look for various ways to approach the city.

By the end of April, when the roads were nearly dry, Grant moved his army south of Vicksburg on the opposite bank of the river. On April 30, the Union army, assisted by the navy, began to cross the river from Louisiana to Bruinsburg, Mississippi. Soon Grant had 40,000 men on the Mississippi side of the river. He knew that General John Pemberton had 32,000 Confederate troops in the vicinity of Vicksburg, and that General Joseph E. Johnston was gathering some 16,000 more at Jackson, Mississippi. Grant decided that he would move between these two forces and beat them separately, but he knew that he did not have men to spare to keep open a line of communications to the navy on the river.

Grant now made a daring decision. With only three days' rations, and all the ammunition the men could carry and pack onto carts and wagons, Grant struck off into central Mississippi. He planned to live off the country, moving so fast and hitting so hard that he would be back near the river at Vicksburg before he ran out of ammunition.

Pemberton tried again and again to attack Grant's communications. He discovered too late that Grant had no line of communications. By then, the Union army had fought its way to Jackson, and on May 14, Grant drove Johnston out of the city. Destroying all supplies and manufacturing facilities at Jackson, Grant turned west to deal with Pemberton.

On May 16, the Union advance guard ran into Pemberton's army, about 22,000 men, in a strong defensive position at Champion's Hill. Because of the mistakes of Union General John McClernand, Pemberton was at first successful. But Grant arrived on the field to take personal control and, with 29,000 men, won a complete victory.

On May 17, Grant drove the Southerners from their defensive position at the Big Black River. Next day, his troops were in sight of Vicksburg. They had reached their goal after eighteen days of incessant marching and fighting.

On May 19, Grant tried to capture the city by assault, but Pemberton's troops, behind their fortifications, repulsed the attackers.

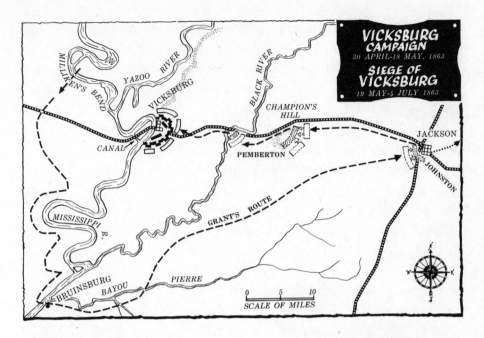

Grant tried again on May 22, but he did not have enough men to overcome the determined, well-protected defenders, so he began a siege of the city.

For more than six weeks, Pemberton, his men, and the citizens of Vicksburg fought on under bombardment from Grant's artillery and from the navy's gunboats. By early July, Pemberton knew that it was hopeless to resist any longer. Food was almost gone; the defenders were eating rats. Pemberton knew that Grant had received reinforcements, and was about to make an attack that would overwhelm the defenders.

On July 3, Pemberton asked for surrender terms. Grant at first demanded unconditional surrender, but then, in recognition of the bravery of the defense, he gave generous terms for feeding the Confederate army, and permitted officers and men to keep their personal belongings.

July 4, the day after Lee's defeat at Gettysburg, Vicksburg surrendered. As 29,500 Confederate soldiers marched out of the city to lay down their arms, Union soldiers cheered them.

More than any other event, the surrender of Vicksburg marked the turning point of the war. In Ulysses S. Grant the Northern people had a general who was comparable to Lee and Jackson.

CHICKAMAUGA AND CHATTANOOGA

September 19–20, November 24–25, 1863

FOR ALMOST SIX months, Rosecrans and his army stayed quietly in Murfreesboro. Grant had expected Rosecrans would help him during the Vicksburg campaign by keeping Bragg busy, but the Union general did so little that Bragg was able to send reinforcements to Pemberton and Johnston. In June, 1863, Rosecrans was active for about one week, and Bragg withdrew from Tullahoma to Chattanooga. But then Rosecrans stopped again, and stayed at Tullahoma nearly two months.

Not until August 16, after the Union government threatened to replace him, did Rosecrans start again, heading for Chattanooga. At the same time General Burnside, with 15,000 Union men, advanced through the Cumberland Gap toward Knoxville.

Pretending to approach Chattanooga from the northwest, Rosecrans actually moved his army south into northern Alabama, then turned to approach the city from the southwest. This unexpected move threatened Bragg's lines of communication along the railroad to Atlanta. On September 7, Bragg abandoned Chattanooga without a fight. Following the retreating Southerners, Rosecrans' army swept eastward into northern Georgia on a front of forty-five miles.

The Confederate government, alarmed by the loss of Chattanooga, sent reinforcements to Bragg. Among these was Longstreet's corps from Virginia. When this corps arrived, Bragg would have 70,000 men. The Confederate general had missed several

71

chances to concentrate against Rosecrans' scattered units, but now with his strengthened army, he turned to fight.

Rosecrans, suddenly realizing that his army was in danger of being gobbled up a bit at a time, frantically tried to bring his forces together. Thanks to Bragg's slowness, he was able to assemble his 60,000 men late on September 18, beside Chickamauga Creek, about ten miles south of Chattanooga.

By now, part of Longstreet's men had arrived to reinforce the Southern army, and Bragg decided to attack next day. He planned to envelop the Union left flank, to cut Rosecrans off from Chattanooga. But the Confederates had trouble coordinating their movement through the wooded, hilly country. Though they came close to victory on September 19, General George H. Thomas on the Union left, was able to hold his position.

During the night, Longstreet and the rest of his men joined Bragg's army, and Bragg changed his plan. He would attack all along the line in the morning, then with the entire Union army engaged, Longstreet's corps on the Confederate left would make the main attack. And due to a mistake by Rosecrans, there was a big gap in the right center of the Union line when Longstreet attacked just before noon.

The whole Union right flank collapsed, and Rosecrans himself was swept back to Chattanooga. Only Thomas' corps stood firm, holding the left. But Longstreet was swinging up from the south, about to cut him off.

Just at this moment, General Gordon Granger, whose small reserve corps had been kept out of the fight by Rosecrans, decided to come to Thomas' assistance. He arrived at Thomas' right flank just in time to meet Longstreet. Then Thomas slowly withdrew

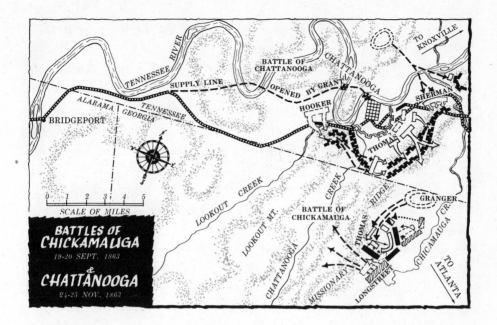

his and Granger's men from the field, putting up a resistance so valiant and so effective that from that time on, Thomas was known as "the Rock of Chickamauga."

Casualties in the battle had been terrible. The Confederates, who had been attacking steadily for two days, lost 18,000. The Union army lost 16,000 and many more were refugees in the wooded mountains south of Chattanooga. Union losses would have been heavier had Bragg pursued.

By September 21, Rosecrans had assembled over 30,000 men in Chattanooga. Bragg slowly followed to the outskirts of the city and ringed it with entrenchments. Then he blocked all the railroads and roads south of the Tennessee River. Though the Union troops held the north bank of the river, autumn rains made the mountain roads impassable for wagons, guns, or large bodies of troops. The Union army in Chattanooga was cut off from all supplies, and it could not get out without fearful losses. Rosecrans' situation was desperate.

At Knoxville, Burnside was not much better off. The Confederates held the railroad, and he couldn't get supplies over the muddy roads through the Cumberland Gap. His army, like Rosecrans', faced starvation.

President Lincoln now appointed Grant to command all forces west of the Appalachians, and directed him to give his personal attention to the critical situations of Rosecrans and Burnside. Grant immediately hurried to Chattanooga, taking a long roundabout trip on muddy mountain trails. On the way, he ordered General Thomas to replace Rosecrans and take command of the Army of the Cumberland.

Arriving on October 23, Grant quietly got the situation under control. He organized a surprise attack which broke through the Confederate units holding the road to Bridgeport. Four days after his arrival, the half-starved men were fed full meals from a wagon supply train which Grant had ordered. With the supplies came two corps of the Army of the Potomac under "Fighting Joe" Hooker.

Even with these reinforcements, Grant had only about 45,000 men, not nearly enough to storm the powerful entrenchments on Missionary Ridge and Lookout Mountain, overlooking Chattanooga. These were held by about 65,000 Confederates, so Grant decided to wait for the arrival of General William Tecumseh Sherman, who was marching east from Vicksburg with about 20,000 men.

Bragg now sent Longstreet and 20,000 men to capture Knoxville from Burnside's weakened army. Bragg was sure his remaining men could hold the lines around Chattanooga against double their number. But Grant thought otherwise, and completed his plans for attack.

Sherman arrived late on November 23, and Grant ordered him to attack the right flank of the Confederate position on Missionary Ridge early next day. At the same time, Hooker was to attack the positions on Lookout Mountain, and then cross Chattanooga Creek to hit the left flank of the Confederates' Missionary Ridge position. Meanwhile Thomas' army was only to demonstrate against the center of the Missionary Ridge line, where the Confederates were strongly entrenched.

Bragg did not have enough men to hold both Lookout Mountain and Missionary Ridge against really determined attacks. Hooker's men climbed Lookout Mountain through a low-lying mist, to win the "Battle Above the Clouds" without much trouble. Sherman, however, was not able to make much progress, as the Confederates were ready for his flank attack. Grant ordered the battle to continue on November 25, following the same plan.

Again Sherman attacked without success. Hooker was delayed, so by mid-afternoon Grant ordered Thomas to attack the first line of trenches in the Confederate position. This would make it easier for Sherman to advance, and would also help Hooker, when he arrived.

Thomas' Army of the Cumberland drove the Southern defenders from the first line of entrenchments at the base of Missionary Ridge. Grant watched this with approval, from a hill in the middle of the plain. Then, to his amazement and annoyance, he saw the troops continue, without an order, following the Southerners up the steep ridge, into the face of the fire from the upper line of entrenchments. Grant had wanted to avoid such a frontal attack.

For two days the Southerners had been watching the great Union army maneuvering over the plain below. Apparently awe-struck by the spectacle, they were frightened as the Northerners dashed up the hill. For the first and only time during the war, Confederate veterans ran from their entrenchments. The cheering Union soldiers swept to the top. They had avenged their defeat at Chickamauga; the entire Confederate army was retreating into the early November dusk.

The Union army lost only 5,800 men in the battle of Chattanooga, while the Confederates lost 6,700. Grant wanted to pursue, but he had been ordered by President Lincoln to do everything in his power to rescue Burnside. He immediately sent Sherman to do this job. Sherman, driving Longstreet from Knoxville, arrived at that city on December 6. East Tennessee was securely in Union hands, and Grant now held the approaches to Georgia and the Carolinas.

WILDERNESS, SPOTSYLVANIA AND COLD HARBOR

May 5–June 3, 1864

On MARCH 3, 1864, President Lincoln appointed Ulysses S. Grant General-in-Chief of the United States Army, giving him complete authority for organizing and directing all Northern forces. For the first time there would be one master plan for all of the Union armies.

Grant realized that only by bringing pressure against the Confederates at all points, and then never letting up, could the North's greater manpower and industrial production win over the courage and determination of the South. General Meade's Army of the Potomac must keep Lee's army engaged in central Virginia. At the same time the Western army, now commanded by Sherman, must

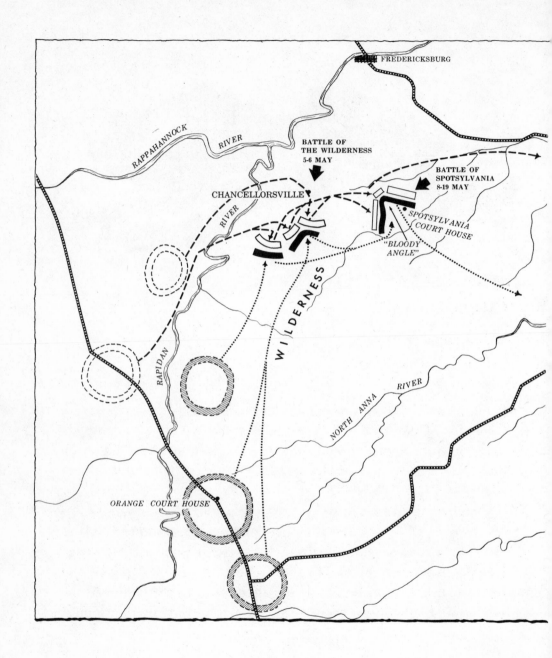

FREDERICKSBURG

RAPPAHANNOCK RIVER

BATTLE OF
THE WILDERNESS
5-6 MAY

BATTLE OF
SPOTSYLVANIA
8-19 MAY

CHANCELLORSVILLE

RIVER

SPOTSYLVANIA
COURT HOUSE

"BLOODY
ANGLE"

RAPIDAN

W I L D E R N E S S

NORTH ANNA RIVER

ORANGE COURT HOUSE

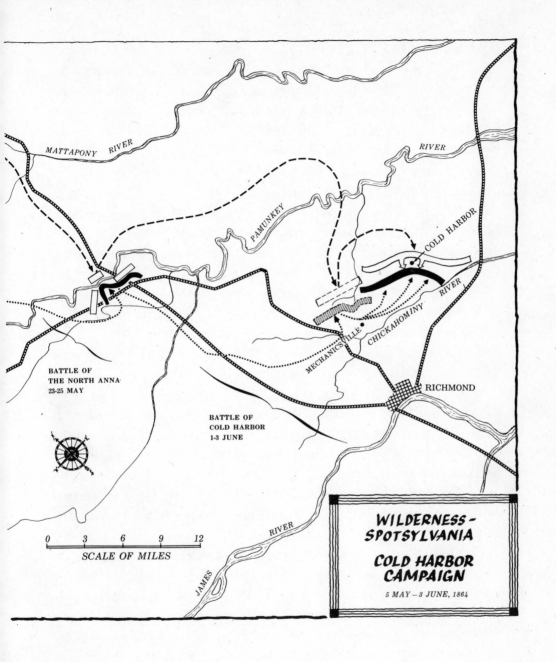

MATTAPONY RIVER

RIVER

PAMUNKEY

COLD HARBOR

CHICKAHOMINY RIVER

MECHANICSVILLE

BATTLE OF
THE NORTH ANNA
23-25 MAY

BATTLE OF
COLD HARBOR
1-3 JUNE

RICHMOND

0   3   6   9   12
SCALE OF MILES

RIVER

JAMES

WILDERNESS-
SPOTSYLVANIA

COLD HARBOR
CAMPAIGN

5 MAY – 3 JUNE, 1864

fight its way from Chattanooga into Georgia and the Carolinas, cutting off the food and other supplies that would otherwise be sent to Lee. Other Union forces must coordinate with these main armies and with each other. It was like the battlefield plans Grant had been making earlier in the war, but this time it was on a gigantic scale, across hundreds of miles.

Grant decided to stay with Meade's army. Lee was the most dangerous opponent and had shown that he could easily upset the plans of uncertain or hesitant generals. Grant realized that he must not let this happen again. Since Meade would only carry out Grant's orders from then on, the Army of the Potomac really became Grant's army.

The objective, Grant told Meade, would always be Lee's army. As soon as the roads were dry enough to move, he planned to envelop Lee's right flank, and keep on enveloping it until the Southern army gave up or was driven back into the mountains where it could get no more supplies.

When the fighting began, early in May, Lee realized at once that he could not take chances against this man, as he had with other Union generals. From now on he fought with the utmost caution, but perhaps even more brilliantly than before. Grant, for his part, had great respect for Lee, though he was the first of Lee's opponents who did not fear the great Virginian. Here were two of the greatest generals in history fighting each other to a standstill.

Lee had the advantage of being on the defensive, fighting in country he knew. As Grant tried to circle him, Lee could shift his men more quickly on inside lines, and thus partly equalize the difference in manpower. Grant had the advantage of more men, more and better equipment, and the support of a great industrial country to keep him always supplied.

At the beginning of May, Lee's army, 64,000 strong, was concentrated west of Chancellorsville, below the Rapidan River. Grant's army, 119,000 men, lay just to the north, mostly in the area between the Rappahannock and Rapidan rivers. On May 4 the Northerners started moving, crossing the Rapidan just northwest of Chancellorsville, as Hooker had done a year earlier.

The dense tangle of forest and underbrush which the Union army was now entering was known as the Wilderness. Lee had shown at Chancellorsville that a few determined men could hold off a much greater number in this wild region, where any movement off the roads was difficult. Therefore, he promptly engaged the Northerners in battle early on May 5, about five miles west of Chancellorsville.

This was the beginning of a desperate two-day battle. Though both sides came close to breaking through at different times, at the end of the second day the lines were almost exactly where they had been when Lee started the battle.

Both sides lost heavily—14,000 Southerners and 18,000 Northerners were killed or wounded. But Lee knew that he had started with only half as many men as Grant, and he could not afford such battles unless the Northerners lost twice as many men as he did. From that time on, there were no more of the wild Confederate charges that had won battles like Second Manassas and Chancellorsville.

On May 7 both armies, exhausted, remained in their positions, but that night Grant's men quietly left their trenches and started marching east, then south. Grant was not going to let himself be stopped by a drawn battle—he was going to advance again, trying to envelop Lee's right flank.

But Lee had guessed what Grant would do, and was ready. He marched his army southeastward that same night, and as Grant's men approached Spotsylvania Courthouse at dawn, they ran into Confederates entrenched on both sides of the road.

This was the start of another terrible battle, as Grant sent his men probing through the dense woods to try to find the Southern right flank. Particularly hard fighting took place in the center of Lee's line, where it jutted in a point into the Union positions. The Northerners soon called this point the Bloody Angle. Finally, on May 11, Grant noticed that Lee, to protect his right flank, had weakened the force holding the Bloody Angle. At 4:30 A.M., the next morning, the Northerners attacked there and broke through. But Lee quickly established another line just behind it, and both sides were too tired to continue the battle.

Once more Lee had been able to stop Grant, but not to defeat him. Again, the Northerners had suffered more losses than the Confederates—but not enough more; Lee had about 12,000 casualties, Grant about 14,000.

There was more fighting at Spotsylvania on May 18 and 19. Grant again tried to get around Lee's right flank, but neither side could gain an advantage, and Grant decided to find a new battlefield. On the night of May 20 he again started south. Lee was alert and ready. Once again his men made a rapid night march and reached the crossings of the North Anna River, just before the Northerners.

This time Grant did not try a major attack. Finding no weaknesses in Lee's positions, he moved south, around Lee's right, on the evening of May 26. The Union army was near the old Mechanicsville battlefield before it was stopped once more by Lee on May 30. As before, Grant extended his left flank to get around Lee's right.

On June 2, Grant detected a weakening of Lee's center, as the Southerner extended his right flank to the Chickahominy River just below Cold Harbor. Grant decided to attack the weak spot on June 3.

Grant's attack started at dawn, only to be met by a murderous hail of artillery and small arms fire. Lee had received reinforcements during the night, and guessing Grant's plans, had thrown the fresh troops into the vital spot. In an hour, the attackers lost 7,000 men without making the slightest impression on the defenders. Grant called off the attack. Lee had gained his first clear-cut victory over Grant. In the three-day Battle of Cold Harbor, he had lost only 3,000 men. Grant had had 13,000 casualties.

The South hoped that Grant would admit defeat, as other Union generals had under similar circumstances. But clear-sighted Lee feared that this man would not give up so easily.

TO ATLANTA AND THE SEA

May 4–December 21, 1864

ON MAY 4, 1864, as Grant was pressing into the Wilderness, Sherman's army began to march southward from Chattanooga toward Atlanta, one of the most important industrial cities of the South. Sherman's force really consisted of three small armies: General Thomas' Army of the Cumberland, 61,000 strong; General James B. McPherson's Army of the Tennessee, 24,000 men; and General John M. Schofield's Army of the Ohio, 14,000 strong.

Twenty-five miles southeast of Chattanooga, holding a line across the main railroad near Dalton, Georgia, lay General "Joe" Johnston's army of 50,000 Southerners.

Johnston, who had replaced General Bragg after Chattanooga, had been given the task of trying to stop an invasion by an army

84

twice as large as his own, with superior weapons and equipment.

This was the beginning of another contest between two brilliant, equally-matched generals. Johnston realized that he could not stop Sherman immediately, but he could delay him and make him use up his strength. The further south Sherman went, the more men he would need to hold his line of communications back to Chattanooga. But as Johnston fell back, he would be able to get his supplies more quickly from Atlanta, and from the fertile farms of central Georgia. He hoped by skillful delaying tactics to so weaken the Union army that the strength of the two armies would be even, some time before reaching Atlanta.

Sherman knew just what Johnston had in mind. Therefore, as he moved south, he avoided attacking strong Confederate positions where a few men could stop large numbers and cause the attackers many casualties.

When Sherman moved up to Johnston's defenses west of Dalton early in May, he detached only a small part of his army to hold the front of the Southern army. With the bulk of his troops he swung westward to start a turning movement around the Confederate left flank. Johnston promptly fell back to another strong position near Resaca. On May 15 Sherman did the same thing as before, and Johnston fell back to Cassville, only to be forced out again on May 19 by another of Sherman's turning movements.

This happened again at Allatoona on May 23. The Northerners started around to the west, expecting that Johnston would again fall back along the railroad. Instead, Johnston marched rapidly south, then west, to take up a position right in the path of the main Union army, about ten miles west of the railroad at Marietta.

Sherman now tried to move around Johnston's right, toward the

85

railroad. But the Southerner took up strong positions on the hills north of Marietta, once more blocking the railroad. Now came three weeks of maneuvering, as Sherman tried to force Johnston out of these positions without fighting a big battle. Union officers and men began to grumble that they could drive the Southerners out with a frontal attack, so on June 27 Sherman tried an assault on Kenesaw Mountain. When Johnston repulsed it, Sherman's men began to see that their commander was right, and there was no more grumbling about the long marches he made them take.

Sherman now made another turning movement west of Marietta, and once more Johnston was forced back, this time to the line of the Chattahoochee River. On July 8, Sherman made an unexpected crossing of the Chattahoochee around the Confederate right, and Johnston was again forced back—this time to Peach Tree Creek, on the very outskirts of Atlanta.

At last Johnston made ready for the big battle which he expected would save Georgia. He had made Sherman take seventy-four days to go one hundred miles, and had compelled him to detach large forces to protect his lengthening line of communications. Now both armies were nearly the same fighting strength and Johnston planned to strike boldly the next time Sherman tried to make a move around his flank. But he was never to have a chance. President Davis was dissatisfied with Johnston's retreating, and on July 17, replaced him with General John Bell Hood.

Hood got ready to attack at the first opportunity. This came on July 20, when Sherman began to cross Peach Tree Creek and swing east of Atlanta. Hood thought he saw an opportunity to overwhelm the Union right flank, commanded by Thomas. While part of his army was holding off the rest of the Union army, Hood

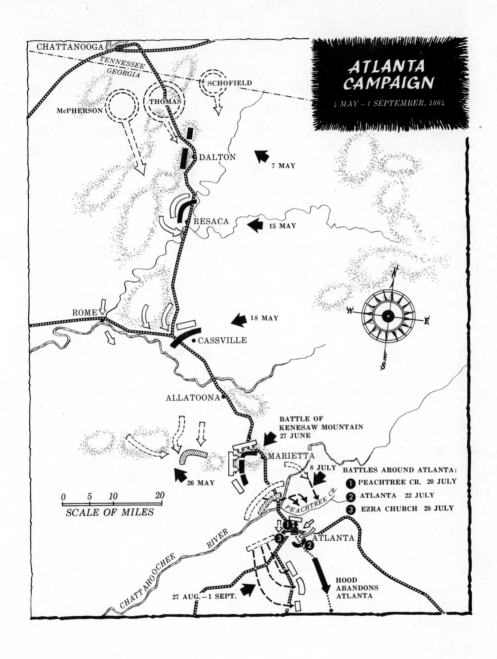

CHATTANOOGA

TENNESSEE
GEORGIA

SCHOFIELD

McPHERSON   THOMAS

ATLANTA
CAMPAIGN

4 MAY – 1 SEPTEMBER, 1864

DALTON

7 MAY

RESACA

15 MAY

ROME

18 MAY

CASSVILLE

N
W   E
S

ALLATOONA

BATTLE OF
KENESAW MOUNTAIN
27 JUNE

MARIETTA

8 JULY

BATTLES AROUND ATLANTA:

1 PEACHTREE CR. 20 JULY

2 ATLANTA 22 JULY

3 EZRA CHURCH 28 JULY

26 MAY

0   5   10   20

SCALE OF MILES

PEACHTREE CR.

3   ATLANTA

CHATTAHOOCHEE   RIVER

27 AUG. – 1 SEPT.

HOOD
ABANDONS
ATLANTA

led an attack of 20,000 against Thomas, but was repulsed with heavy losses.

As Sherman continued to close in east of Atlanta, Hood noticed that the left flank of the Union army was unprotected. This time he attacked with greatly superior numbers, and surprised Sherman completely. Union General McPherson was killed, and the Union left flank fell back. But Sherman quickly reinforced them, and the Northerners turned on the Southerners with a surprise counterattack. Hood was thrown back with 8,000 casualties. The Northerners lost only 3,700. Hood, in his first two battles with Sherman, had lost twice as many men. He withdrew into the defenses of Atlanta.

Sherman saw that he didn't have enough men to attack these fortifications successfully, nor enough to surround the city. He decided he would go around to the west to try to draw Hood into another battle, and then, if possible, to get south of the city to cut the railroad lines.

On July 28, Hood made another desperate attack at Ezra Church, west of Atlanta. Sherman was waiting for him, and lost only 600 men, while Hood lost 4,300. Then Sherman maneuvered gradually around southwest of Atlanta. Striking suddenly late in August, he cut the two main railroad lines into the city. Hood had to abandon Atlanta, and Sherman marched in.

Moving north of Atlanta, Hood tried to cut Sherman's line of communications. Sherman followed for a while, then realized that if he chased Hood he would not be carrying out Grant's plan of keeping constant presusre on the South. He returned to Atlanta, sending General Thomas to protect Tennessee.

Hood was marching north into Tennessee, but Sherman was

confident that Thomas, "the Rock of Chickamauga," could take care of him. Ignoring what was happening behind him, Sherman abandoned his line of communications, and on November 12, with 60,000 veteran soldiers, marched east from Atlanta to the sea.

Georgians will never forget Sherman's "March to the Sea." The Union soldiers lived off the country, and destroyed every bit of food they couldn't eat, and any other supplies that could have been used by Southern armies. Sherman gave strict orders that Southern women, children, and unarmed men should not be hurt. Though the Southerners hated him for devastating their property, he was only doing his duty as a soldier. He had been ordered to destroy the ability of the South to fight, just as rapidly and completely as he could. He did his job thoroughly.

On December 10, Sherman reached the sea near Savannah, linked up with the Union navy, and on December 21, captured Savannah.

Meanwhile, Hood was trying to bring back Southern control in Tennessee. Driving rapidly north, he was checked on November 30, by General Schofield at the Battle of Franklin, but despite heavy losses, pressed on to try to capture Nashville. There General Thomas was assembling a new Union army. At the same time he also managed to keep Hood occupied outside of Nashville. Then, on December 15 and 16, Thomas attacked, and completely destroyed the Southern army.

Hood had done just what he had tried to avoid. He had made it easy for Sherman to overrun Georgia, and he had made certain that Tennessee would remain under Northern control. His disasters at Atlanta and at Nashville were blows from which the South would never recover.

PETERSBURG TO APPOMATTOX

June 15, 1864–April 9, 1865

THOUGH GRANT was as sad about the loss of lives in his assault at Cold Harbor as Lee had been after Pickett's Charge, he could not let his sorrow make him forget his duty as a soldier. He was determined to continue the pressure against the South.

On the morning of June 13 the Southern soldiers at Cold Harbor woke in their trenches to find that the Union army had disappeared during the night. Because one Union corps was approaching Richmond from the east, Lee thought at first that Grant had simply moved south of the Chickahominy. Lee hurried to the vicinity of the old Malvern Hill battlefield to take new positions in front of this supposed threat. While Lee's men were entrenching, the rest of Grant's army was crossing the James River, partly by boat, and partly by a great ponton bridge, almost half a mile long. This was the only time during the war that Lee was completely fooled by an opponent.

Grant hoped to be able to take advantage of the favorable position of the army of Union General Benjamin F. Butler, on the south bank of the James River. Butler's small army had been sent by boat up the James to attack Richmond early in May, and to cut Lee's line of communications. This move was intended to be coordinated with Grant's advance into the Wilderness. But when Butler landed at Bermuda Hundred, between Richmond and Petersburg, he was stopped by a force less than half the strength of his own, commanded by General Beauregard. For a month But-

90

ler's army stayed bottled up on the peninsula at Bermuda Hundred.

Now, as the Army of the Potomac was starting across the James River, Grant knew that if Butler could seize Petersburg quickly, Lee's army in Richmond would be completely cut off from the rest of the South. Grant sent reinforcements by boat to Butler, and ordered him to advance against Petersburg on both sides of the Appomattox River. Beauregard had only about 10,000 men. Even Butler shouldn't fail with more than 30,000.

But Butler *did* fail. So did General W. F. Smith, sent by Butler to attack Petersburg with 16,000 men on June 15. When the 2,400 defenders opened fire, Smith stopped and waited for reinforcements. Then, when Beauregard rushed to Petersburg with most of his men, Butler poked out of his position at Bermuda Hundred, but one Confederate division was enough to send Butler scurrying back to his old trenches.

Grant ordered an attack on Petersburg on June 16. But Beauregard's men, though greatly outnumbered, were protected by carefully prepared fortifications. They repulsed the attacks. Early on June 18, after most of his army had arrived, Grant tried again. By this time Lee had reached Petersburg, and the Union soldiers were thrown back again.

Though he had failed to win the great victory he had expected, Grant knew that he now had Lee in a very tight spot. With part of his army holding Lee's men practically in a siege in the entrenchments around Petersburg and Richmond, Grant began swinging part of his army south of Petersburg to cut the vital railway supply lines. Lee of course realized this danger, and so there followed a series of desperate battles for control of these railroads.

It was slow, tough work, and both generals did their best to avoid attacking where they would lose many men. But Grant held most of the advantages. He received reinforcements, while Lee's men grew tired. During the summer, fall, and winter, Grant slowly extended his lines westward below Petersburg, while Lee stretched his defensive lines ever thinner.

Late in the summer, the Northerners made one more effort to seize Petersburg itself. A regiment of Pennsylvania coal miners dug a deep tunnel under the Confederate trenches. This mine was then filled with gunpowder and exploded, tearing a great gap in the defending line of entrenchments. Union troops were supposed to dash through this opening to capture the town. But General Burnside was slow in ordering his men to attack. When they finally moved, the Confederates had recovered from their surprise and were ready. They stopped the advance, inflicting severe losses on the Union troops trying to get through the mine crater. Grant was very angry at Burnside's slowness, and removed him from his command.

Lee, meanwhile, tried to weaken Grant's grip on Petersburg by sending General Jubal Early to the Shenandoah Valley to create a diversion. Early did a splendid job. He defeated several Union commanders with much larger forces, and gained complete control of the Valley. Then, with about 13,000 men, he made a daring invasion of Maryland, marched to the outskirts of Washington, and attacked its fortifications. Grant sent two corps to help defend the capital, and Early was driven back to the Shenandoah Valley.

Grant now sent General Philip Sheridan with an army of about 40,000 men to the Valley. Sheridan was one of the best Union generals. Though outnumbered two-to-one, Early fought bril-

92

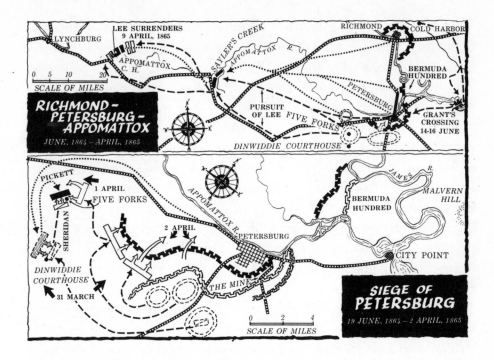

liantly, and on October 19 at Cedar Creek made a surprise attack that was almost successful. But Sheridan, "twenty miles away," galloped up, and saved the day. Early had already done more than most men could have done. He was doomed to fail against an equally good general with greater forces.

After clearing the Valley, Sheridan rejoined Grant at Petersburg early in 1865. Meanwhile, there were many smaller operations going on around the dwindling Confederacy as other Union generals followed Grant's orders to keep up pressure on the South.

Sherman had started north from Savannah and marched through South Carolina, destroying food and property as he had done in Georgia. The South once more called on "Joe" Johnston. Only this time he had few of the troops he had used so well against Sherman the summer before. Though Johnston slowed Sherman down, by March the Union advance had penetrated well into North Carolina, and Johnston knew he must soon surrender.

Back at Petersburg Grant was increasing his pressure on Lee, even though the roads were still in terrible shape from winter and spring rains. Only one railroad line, running westward from Petersburg to Lynchburg, was left open. The Union army, spearheaded by Sheridan's cavalry corps, moved toward it. On March 31, Lee sent Pickett on a daring flank attack. Pickett struck Sheridan unexpectedly near Dinwiddie Courthouse, but the Union troops forged ahead and next day, at Five Forks, overwhelmed Pickett's corps.

On April 2, while Sheridan pushed ahead to the railroad, the Union army assaulted the center of the Confederate line south of Petersburg. By this time the tired defenders were spread too thin, and could not stop the Northerners. Lee knew that he could no longer hold Richmond and Petersburg, but he was not ready to give up the fight. In one last desperate effort he took most of his army and rapidly marched west, hoping to get away to join Johnston. The Confederate government fled Richmond, just before Union troops entered the city.

Grant immediately pursued. Lee had left Ewell with a rear guard at Sayler's Creek, but they were quickly overwhelmed on April 7. Grant sent Sheridan's cavalry to cut off Lee's escape to Lynchburg. On April 8, Sheridan, blocking the escape route, stopped the Southerners near Appomattox Courthouse.

In his last battle, Lee came close to breaking through Sheridan's

94

lines, but Grant was coming up behind too fast. Though his men begged him to order one more charge, Lee could not send them to their deaths in a cause he knew was hopeless. He sent word to Grant that he was ready to surrender.

Next day, the two great generals met in the parlor of a little house in the village of Appomattox Courthouse. After a brief conversation, Grant wrote out generous surrender terms. The Confederate officers and men could keep their personal belongings, and, as Grant said to Lee, he would "let all men who claim to own a horse or mule take the animals home to work their little farms."

In reply, Lee said that such liberal terms would "have the best possible effect upon the men," and would help to heal the wounds of war. Then, after Grant ordered food sent to Lee's hungry army, the two soldiers parted. As Lee rode away, Grant saluted his brave enemy. Lee, showing how much he appreciated an able, generous foe, returned the salute, and rode off to join his men.

The Civil War was over.

INDEX

(C) *denotes a Confederate general.* (U) *denotes a Union general.*